Sascha Braunig

Sascha Braunig

FOXY PRODUCTION

CONTENTS

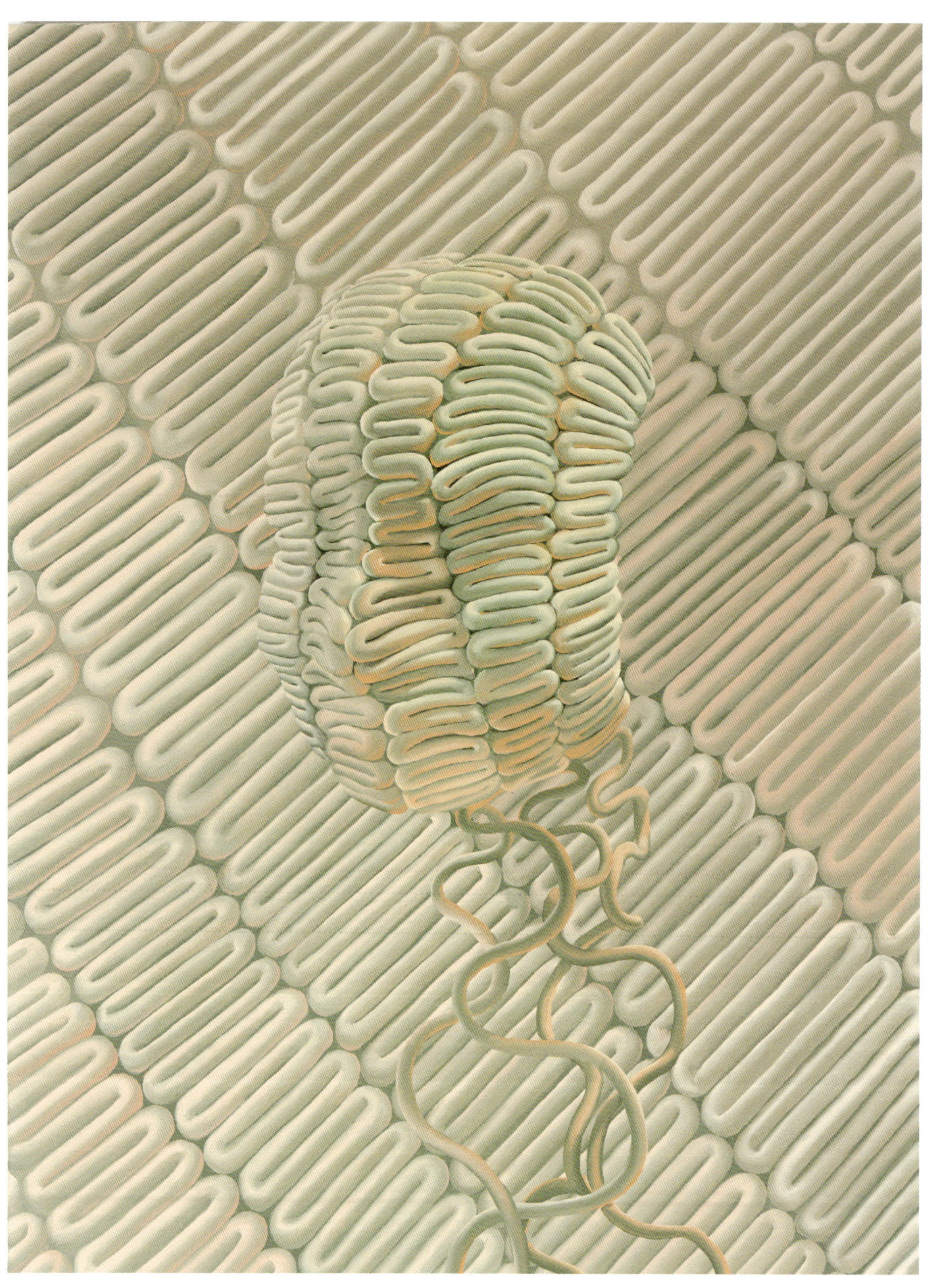

Some Hot Contagion

Sarah Lehrer-Graiwer

A

What fucked up, irresistibly nightmarish dream world is this? Into what surreal spaceship have we been transported, waking up sticky and trapped in a shallow, garish space of indeterminate scale? What awful foresight do these denatured noggins possess, ever cryptic, ever delphic? What manner of masking, what psychological reprogramming is hypothesized? What epidemic do such visions portend, and what future do they figure? Forgive my creeping panic when I fret a bit about what these pictures might be preparing us for. So many red flags.

Still, what's alarming about these paintings is not entirely threatening, not by a long shot. Seduction[1] is the name of this game being played on my retinae. Paint brush wielded as secret stun gun. And I'm melting from too many sublethal, bliss-point visual shocks Sascha Braunig's paintings deliver; leave a body wet all over.

Which is also to say, I'm rather worried by these paintings and their ambiguously anthropomorphic subjects. Worried—that condition of concern well-suited to our moment—but also optimistic about bodies and the way they are redefined and reimagined here. As dissolute, disturbed, and distorted as the figures depicted here are—morphed to the brink of recognition and beyond, stunned into a state of being neither dead nor alive but perhaps undead and seemingly blind—the head and a piercing sense of its headiness persists throughout. Facial features alternately emerge into exquisite sharpness or recede abstractly into masses of small bubbles or a cloud of X chromosomes or even just a trail of rippling energy. Mirror-like in framing, cropping, and scale, we see shattered, spectral suggestions of ourselves—the modernizing 'human'—in these pictures which slyly equate self and painted surface, self and the body excessively adorned, self and the body blown to smithereens.

L

Truth is, portraiture is on the verge of collapse. Despite or precisely because of selfie-mania, the genre balances on increasingly shaky ground, vacillating in an on-again, off-again flirtation with the prospect of its own obliteration, its own obsolescence. The collective death drive rages, in full heat. Can we imagine a time when pictures of ourselves begin to lose relevance? It seems Braunig's creatures can't decide whether or not they even want to exist in our world, to say nothing of their skepticism of humankind as a model species. Yes, there are portrayals of several gloriously cold and severe heads with refined features and smooth skin. Some are self-portraits painted from casts of the artist's face, others are based on friends' faces. Placid, blank, closed-mouth expressions are set in various tones: icy, fierce, and serene. Meticulous but not quite raw or specific, the features tend toward the abstracted and the exaggerated, the ethereal and the pixie. Collectively, the faces Braunig paints describe a certain archetypal Ur-face that is open-endedly gendered, androgynous with strong feminine tendencies and innate glamor. If the type is hermaphroditic, it would be so in the sense of herms, the ancient Greek and Roman sculptures that demarcated a crossroads or trans-zone and were originally devoted to the phallic god Hermes but, as Braunig has noted, "became a genre that could depict other gods,"[2] including female ones. Because as much as these are maximalist oil paintings, they are also about sculpture and senses of mass.

In classic bust tradition, Braunig paints heads mostly in three-quarter view, as well as profiles and a couple rare head-on frontal stares that drive home the whole death-mask vibe that already lurks in the corners. Several early works show the backs of 'heads' (if we can call them that), opened up by deep and wide excavations to expose textured interiors. And, then there are the eyes, the terrible eyes. With each hard and bloated ball she renders, Ariel's mournful fairy song grows louder: "Full fathom five thy father lies; / Of his bones are coral made; / Those are pearls that were his eyes; / Nothing of him that doth fade / But doth suffer a sea-change / Into something rich and strange. Sea-nymphs hourly ring his knell."[3]

There's lots of veiling, cloaking, shrouding, and obscuring going on: a headsock, a wire cage, a studded skintight leather-mommy mask. One day the head looks or feels like a plaster doll-like mannequin, another day an effusion of noodles or a cable-knit sweater or a geyser of wriggling green worms. How to read the features of *Chur*, 2014 (pp. 6 & 73), an expressive mass of tightly wound gray matter that's starting to unravel? Or *Squirm*, 2014 (p. 69), which describes the shape of a sore thumb or gearshift or drumstick as much as anything, having no front or back or apparent sense organs. Often the categories of portrait and person barely hold at all: if portraiture, then also (and even more so) still-life in a way that raises suspicion around notions of head and face. I also harbor doubts about the things I most desire, call it the self-defense of an advertised-to-death being.

I

Instability and mutability of genre—portraiture versus still-life—echoes the morphic challenges Braunig brings to bear on human anatomy and the very ability to recognize something as alive. The human form is a launching pad for so much more, like the theorization of its future mutations, attenuated hybrid bodies, other species real and imagined, and, naturally, aliens. As predictions of mass extinctions dumbfound us, never has the consideration of biological alterity seemed so pressing and necessary. While some of Braunig's more dematerialized and ambiguous shapes conjure other life forms—extraterrestrial or deep sea marine life, or psychosexual dream life—perhaps what's more alien is the nature of vision being proposed, the manner through which figuration and visibility happens. I see a strangeness of seeing, a curiosity about trying to see people, heads, figures, and space take a non-human form or exist in a post-human manner. We try to stretch past our physiological limits and wonder how other creatures see. Is their blue our blue? Do fish really have fish-eye lens? What might we look like to something seeing us for the first time? Do you also feel that intense desire to burst your seams, to get out of this skin, to trade it for another one, a brighter one?

And yet the pictures always look so *real* and blunt. Uncanny, the way color and form seem hyperbolic, unreasonable, totally imagined and outlandish and at the same time are rendered hyper real, 'photographic', immediate. Fantasy is not opposed to material reality and direct sense perception. Rather it is rooted in studio-bound, tabletop concreteness and the painstaking observation of small models constructed by the artist in real space, often in clay, in order to study light on dimensional surfaces. As far-fetched and flamboyantly speculative as the imagery gets, these paintings maintain a fundamental allegiance to the real, the physical, and the concrete that makes their propositions stranger still. Adapting the trompe l'oeil and Dutch still-life tradition, Braunig explains, "Making 3D models to paint from is a 'backstage' sculptural practice that informs the paintings with a tensile materiality even as their imagery appears fantastical. Though I often supplement my observations with invented embellishments and backdrops, the paintings' basis in real light conditions superficially convinces the eye."[4] She captures passages of illumination, radiance, and crisp reflection that are hauntingly lifelike. The clarity is astounding. Such mad skills as an oil painter are not just a matter of virtuosity, they deliver me into an extreme, intimate proximity with weird, jarring, psychedelic scenarios. Illusionism queers the picture plane—surfaces seem to peel away, shred into ribbons, pour over the frame or pull taut like a leather harness. Yanking at its chains, figuration strains beyond representation, stretching for the thrill of disbelief and ecstatic self-doubt.

E

Space is shallow and compressed like a portrait studio backdrop or low-relief altar: the folds of hanging fabric, the receding corner of a table, fluting, piping, curling paper, concavity, and shadow. Flat but not screen-flat, the lush treatment of light-on-things-in-the-world pretty much reroutes most digital associations. The impression is more dioramatic, kind of like looking into a box or through Duchamp's peephole. Things are pushed upfront, rather confrontationally. While her tight framing and cropping is quite pictorial, the dramatic low-tech special effects and sense of space she simulates is very theatrical. The colored gels that illuminate her staged sculptural subjects (and sometimes appear in-frame, attached to clamp lights) are crucial to getting the party started and majorly pump up the volume on form. Lurid and exaggerated, the effect can veer toward the bordello. Earlier works refer to costuming elements like ruffles, grand collars, masks, face paint, and wigs. I think of these as the scary movie paintings. Dressing-up negotiates between self-formation and disguise, revealment and concealment, or as she writes: "Their patterned skins posit a tense intersection between ornament, armor and disfigurement: costume grown into the body itself."[5] More recent works concentrate theatricality in the rippling folds of stage or window curtains, luxuriant and deep, lit from a sharp angle. Painted on elongated supports, thin feelers and prongs comb through columnar ribbing and splayed folds that unfurl from a central axis, like labia.

Nubs and knobs, fingers and breasts, plump sacs and fleshy curves: shadow wraps around woven and interpenetrating forms. There is cushiness and squishiness; upholstered, quilted, and knitted protruberances. Serpentine locks of hair. Balls in sockets and pearly orbs. Plushness and muscular pressure, so palpable. In her paintings, the artist daydreams, "Can figure and frame begin to co-exist in an interweaving, almost erotic relationship? Is this relationship inevitably a sadomasochistic one, with its preconditions of boundaries and control?"[6] For all the deadliness in the paintings, all the mutant pathology and alien morphology, there is also the ghost of Leigh Bowery vogueing in head-to-toe embroidery. And the Countess de Castiglione self-styling with an eye to the future through the time machine of art. This painted world gifts a new kind of naked.

N

For all the reasons that bodies like to be ornamented, interiors want to be decorated. Space is an extension of a body's adorned worldview: an ambulatory aura or an arena to domesticate, turn into one's home, and privately inhabit through customization and décor. Braunig "cannot help but view the patterning and bright colors in my work as a feminization of space."[7] I paint all over my walls, too. Her favorite, recurring patterns are: polka dots; beads, balls, and bubbles; chevron, diagonal, diamond, and zigzag striping; wavy bars, ripples, and dotted-lines. Her favorite textures to paint are: putty, clay, foil, plaster, smooth plastic, skin and painted skin, fine hair, puffy braids and nets. Pattern, texture, and sensational color combine with great vividness and brassy power, pulsing as a unifying field imposed on top of underlying form, or materializing it. Mapping topographies through degrees of distortion, pervasive pattern traces, palpates, and caresses every angle and bulge. Seurat's pointillism shimmers in the atmosphere, a model of painting as a scintillating field, an all-over array of color and atomized mark that covers everything democratically to convey the mutual permeability of things and their environs.

Permeability presents some problems. We see the body bloom into a profusion of beautiful rashes, tumors, pustules, and gilt gold scabs. The face is a metastasized epicenter of aggravated thought—grown over, furrowed, swollen, veined, encrusted and bejeweled like the shell of Des Esseintes's turtle in À Rebours. Necks grow too thin and skulls too narrow. Huge bugged out eyes appear hard as marbles, naked spheres ripe for the plucking—a ball-gag, a giant jawbreaker. The symptoms look weirdly sweet and beguiling, their origin a mystery. Disfigurement never was so appealing, propped up on a crutch like the pink and gold squid mermaid with a long droopy antenna in *Hilt*, 2015 (p. 87). Her disease is gorgeous and enthralling, her affliction sublime—an ornamental trait to bioengineer for. As Dodie Bellamy puts it, "[t]here is no such thing as a hypochondriac; there are only doctors who cannot figure out what is wrong with you."[8]

Braunig describes the condition as a "sickness of space,"[9] casting her all-over patterning as a contagious outbreak. About contagion, she's noted, "…I've painted figures
that could be infecting rather than reflecting their environment."[10] The vision is all
too current: the body contaminating its environment and the environment contaminating the body, caught in a toxic feedback loop with the planet. Form is always
extruded as a secretion or residue of its contingent, sickly conditions; everything is a
riddle of how it came to be. Health is hardly perceptible until sickness sets in; like
silence, it is merely the absence of disturbance. Then illness pinches us awake. When
the sick rule the world, we will say with Bellamy, "I feel so nauseous in my stomach,
this means I'm alive, I am a living being, that I can feel this, and all these sensations
and worries."[11] Hallucinatory sick space argues against timeless purity and static
essences, insisting instead on the inextricability of matter from context (information,
temporality, circumstance, environment). Another way of saying this would be, in
terms drawn from T.J. Clark, that form and figure (you and I) are not nouns but
dynamic processes the way truth must be thought of as a verb—an operation
continually performed in relation to the world.

S

The interpenetration of figure and ground produces camouflage, an aesthetic
engagement that is so deep it's biochemical and libidinal: orienting life toward
syncing systems, matching up, blending in, and melting away in a diffusion of self.
Confusion between visibility and invisibility takes hold like those magic eye
posters from our youth, where the entire image is a buzzing erogenous zone of
razzle dazzle. Any peacock or monarch knows garish optics can prove to be the
best defensive decoys. At the same time, when hyper-visibility rules, as it does, the
few things that remain stubbornly unseen or unfindable become all the more
exciting, that much more important. Technologies of visibility and exposure on a
mass, Big Data scale end up creating the opportunity for invisibility on a micro
scale, getting lost and disappearing amidst the glut of info. Who wouldn't want the
ability to hide effortlessly and observe unselfconsciously, to not be noticed, to avoid
attention, to experience what the world is like when you're not there, to master the
element of surprise. Take *Frotteur*, 2012 (p. 51): hot tangerine and swimming pool
blue-green vibrate like gong waves across the painting. If it were a sound, it would be
full of reverb and pelvicly-felt. A frotteur rubs aggressively—rubbing up against
other bodies, to hell with consent, or rubbing a surface to imprint the textural effects

of its underlying relief. Surface area is maximized by cleft and cleavage. Streaming up out of a plump ponytail, a girlish profile is loosely suggested facing off to the left. The first many times I looked at it, I didn't even notice the best part, the secret surprise— that teasing hand with slender fingers discreetly poking out between the plush ropey folds along the bottom edge. All of a sudden the body is vividly there on the threshold. It's divinely, unexpectedly obscene.

This strategic invisibility or delayed recognition has a feminist sassiness that countermands ego-driven presence and aspires to self-obfuscation, seeking opportunities to exercise collective, indirect influence. Like a ripple effect that morphs as it expands, this kind of energy leaves a trace. Form registers like a shudder passing through different states of matter, from air to glass to water to ice to stone. Bodies are defined by contrasts between substances and changes in temperature, a chill or heat-flash shocking the system. Disguised and hiding in plain sight, camouflage introduces a whiff of suspicion and the excitement of getting away with something—protecting some pertinent sub rosa knowledge. Meanwhile, molded surfaces of every kind are starting to become animate, possibly sentient selves in their own right like some near-future, no-longer-sci-fi virtual reality or artificial intelligence…or just the next generation nano-smartphone.

And again I wonder, what are these images preparing us for?

1. Seduction in the sense described by Baudrillard: "I want thought to be paradoxical, seductive—on condition, clearly, that seduction is not taken to mean flattering manipulation, but a *détournement* of identity, a *détournement* of being." Jean Baudrillard, *Passwords* (London: Verso, 2003): 87.

2. Sascha Braunig, Artist Statement 2015.

3. Shakespeare, *The Tempest* (Act 1, Scene 2: 482-488).

4. Braunig, Artist Statement 2015.

5. Braunig, Artist Statement 2014.

6. Ibid.

7. Ibid.

8. Dodie Bellamy, "When the Sick Rule the World," in *When the Sick Rule the World* (South Pasadena, CA: Semiotext(e), 2015), 34.

9. Braunig, Artist Statement 2015.

10. Braunig, Artist Statement 2014.

11. Bellamy, 29.

Plates

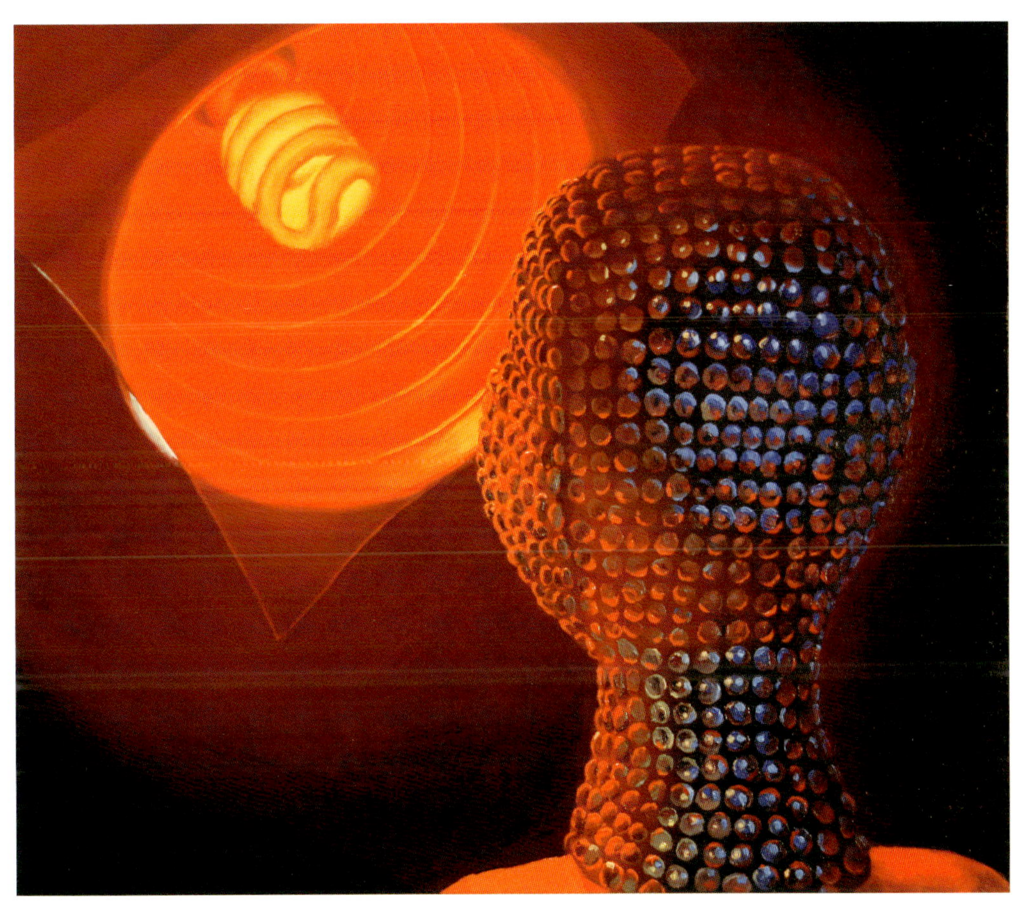

Studs, 2006

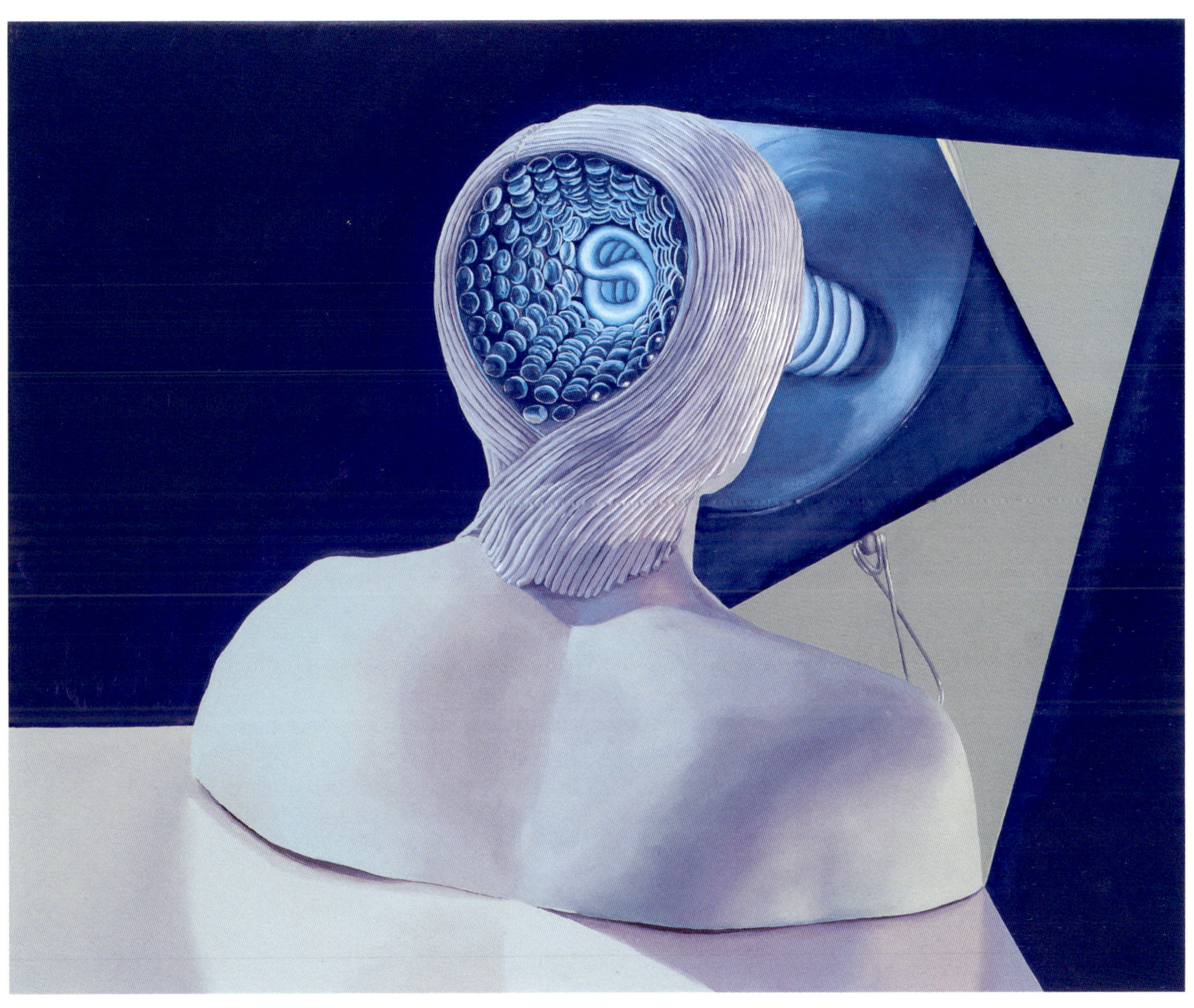

No Solutions, 2009

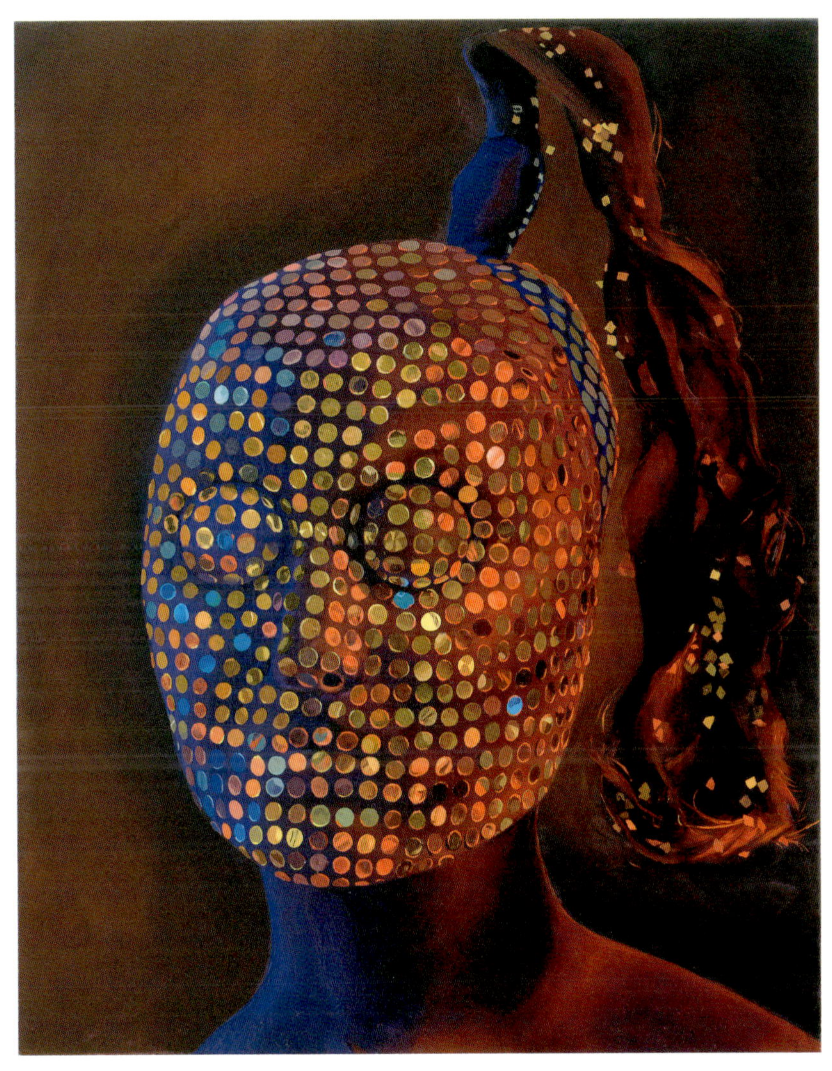

Sequins, 2010

23

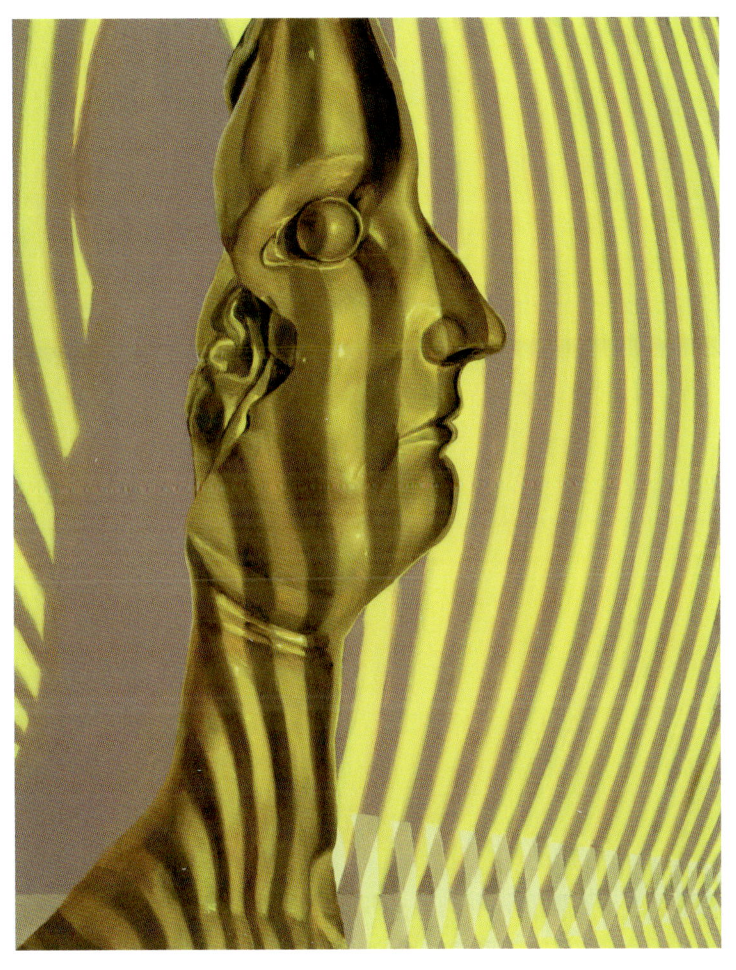

Goldwarp, 2010

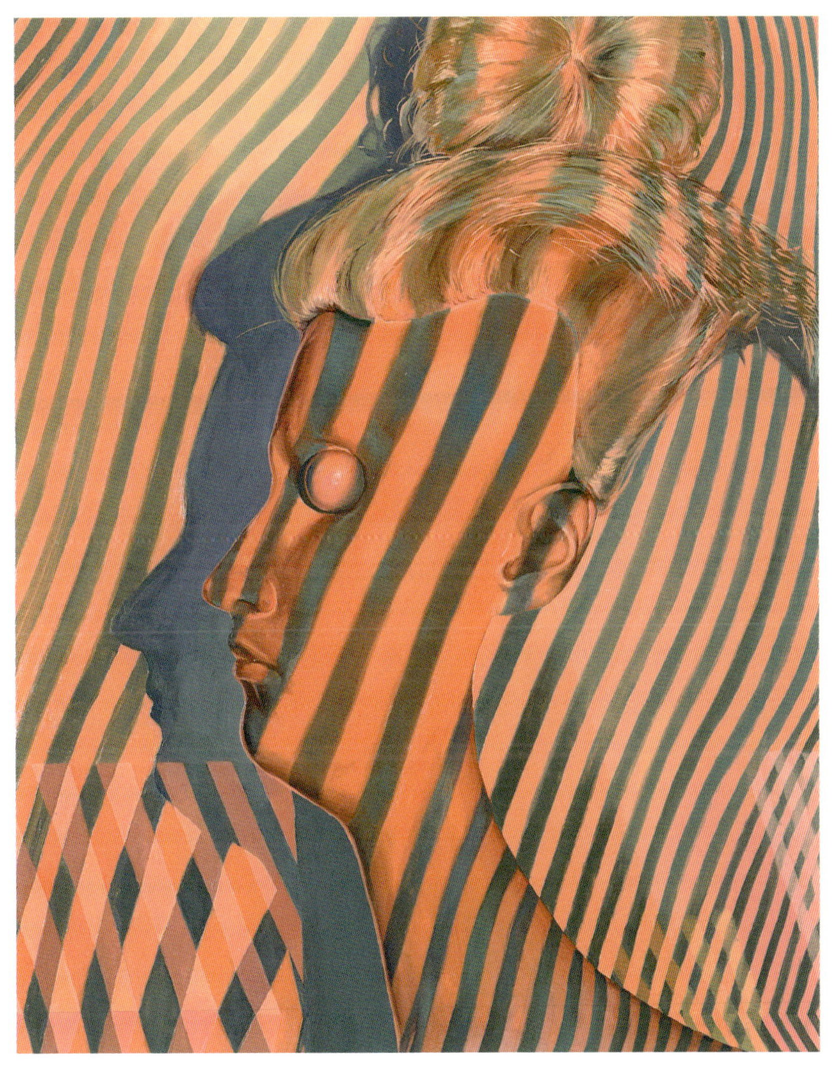

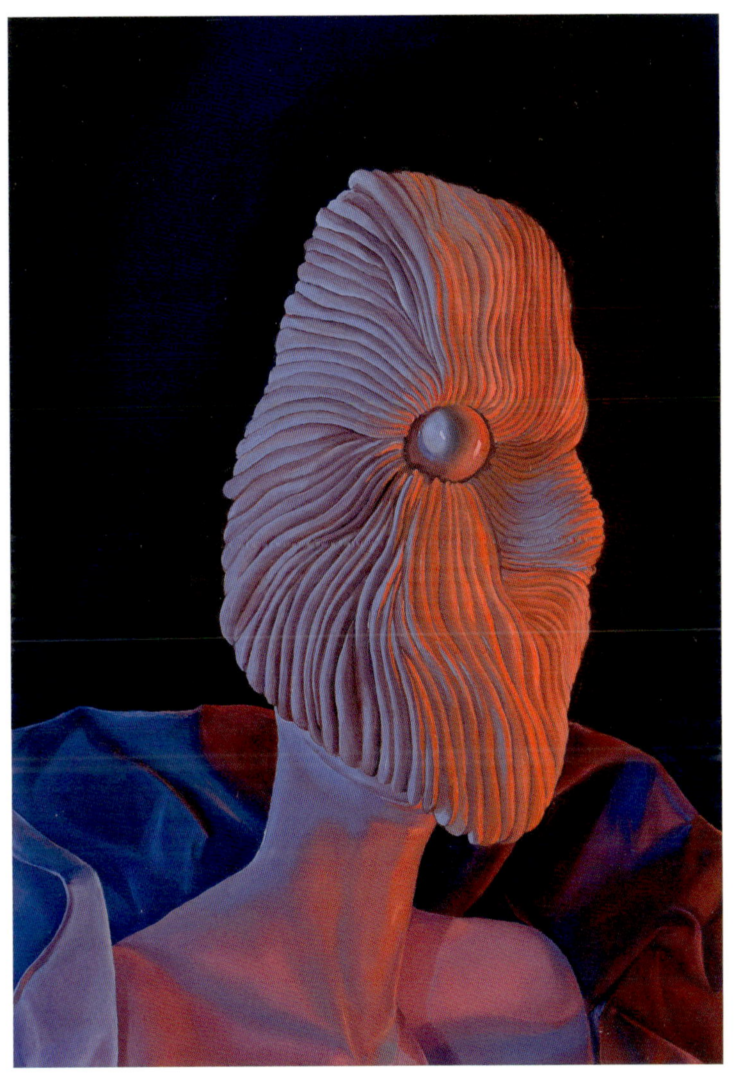

Coverage, 2011

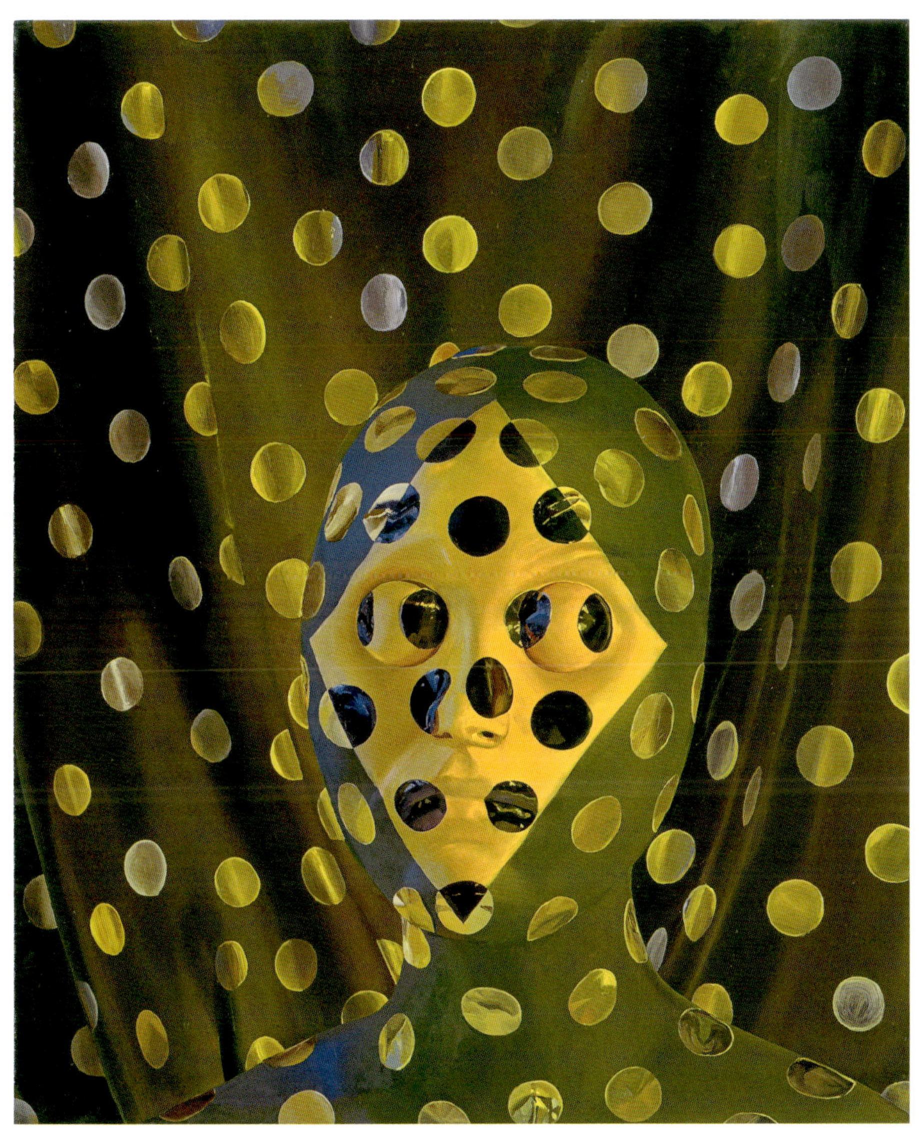

Chameleon, 2011

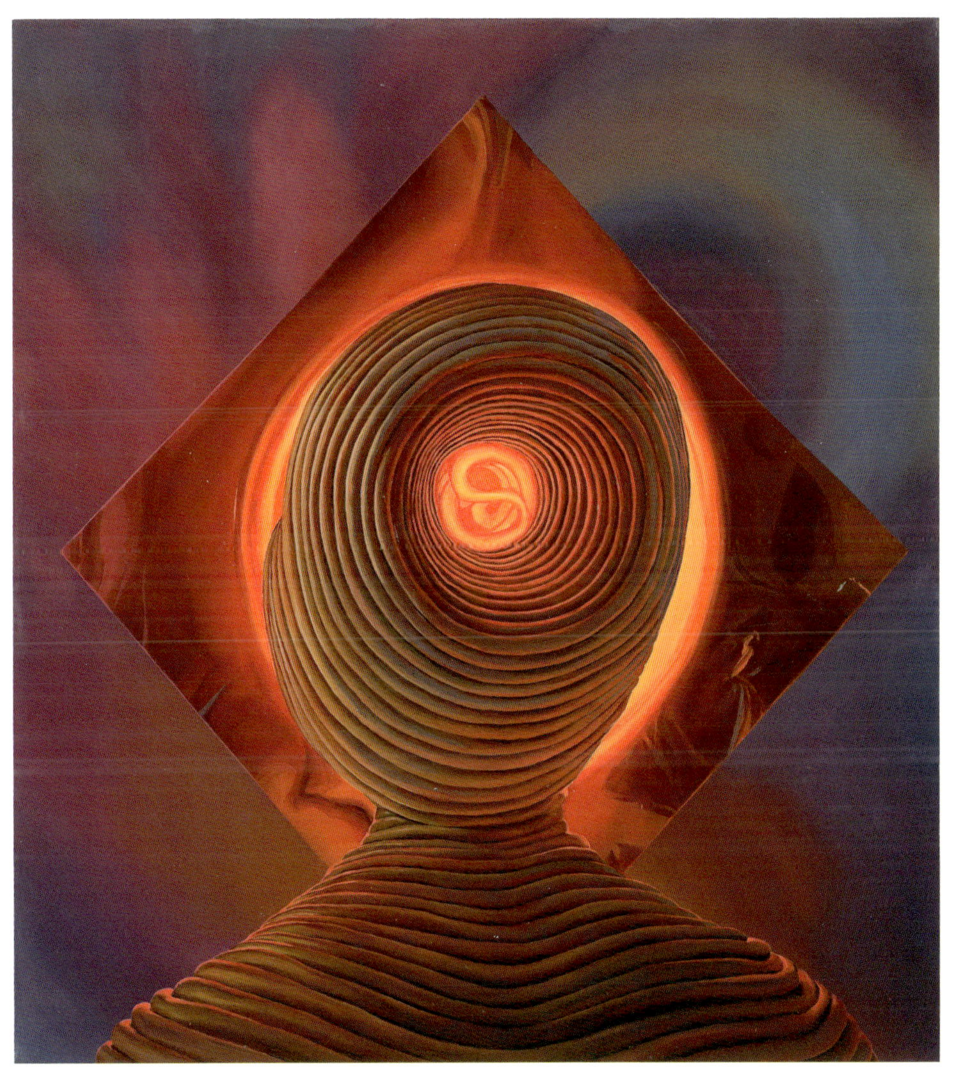

Coils, 2011

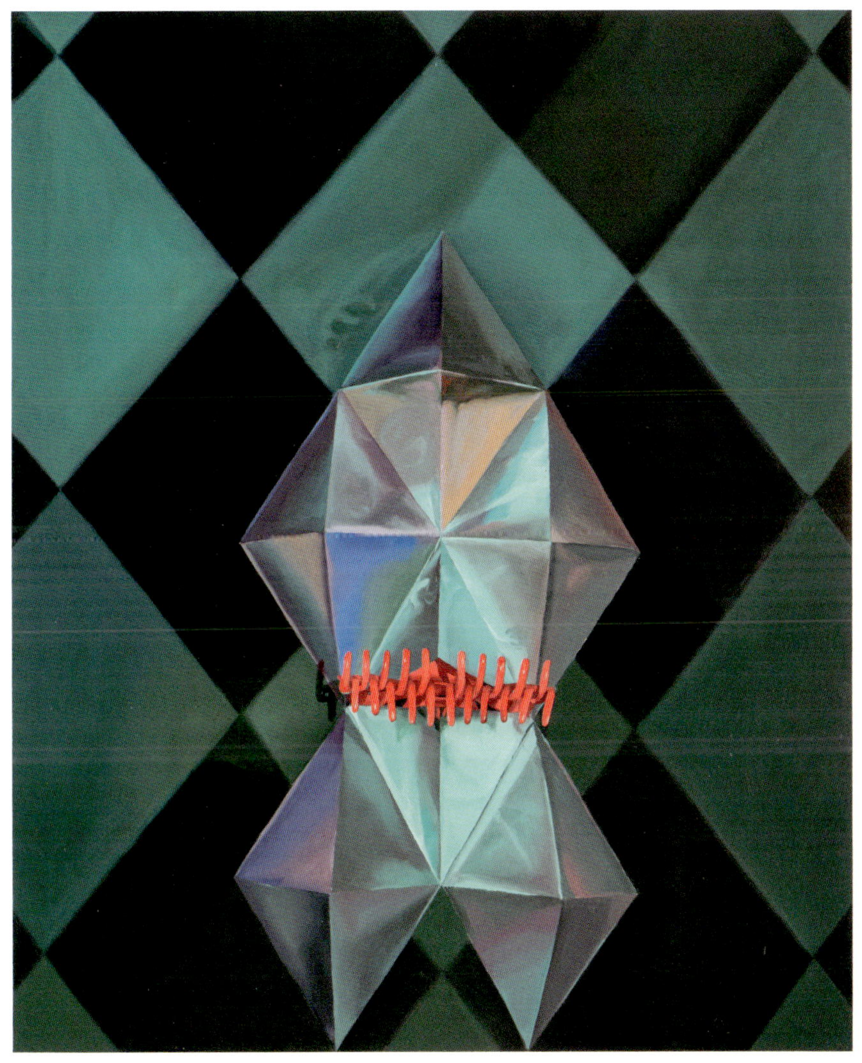

Carapace, 2011

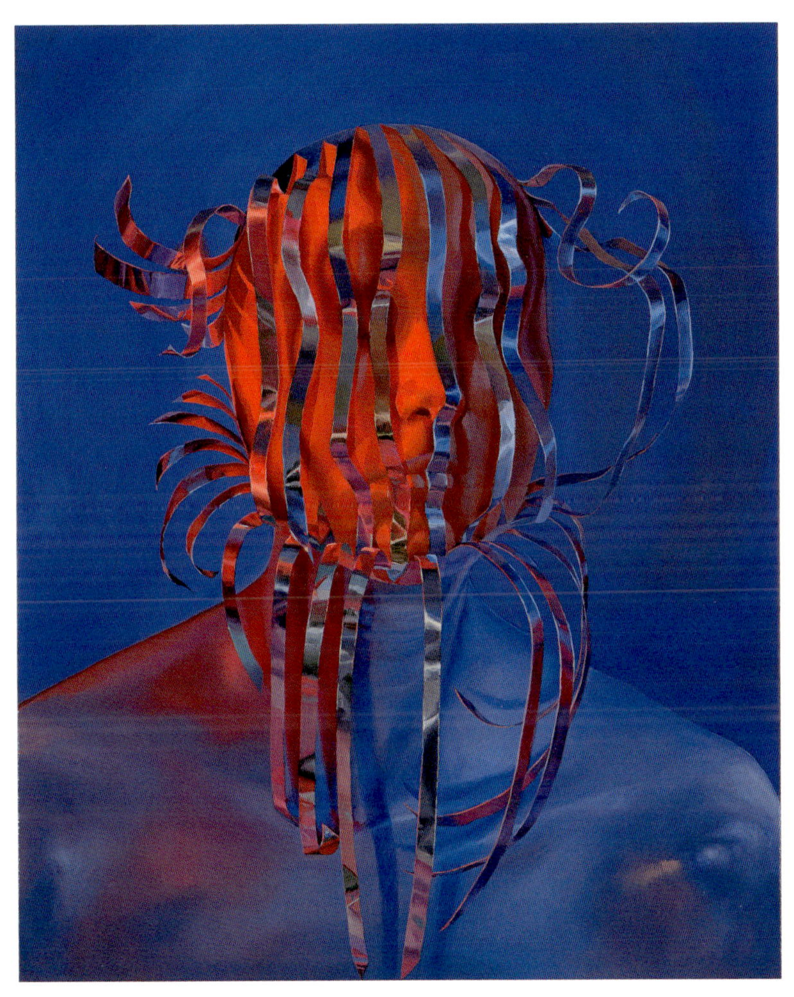

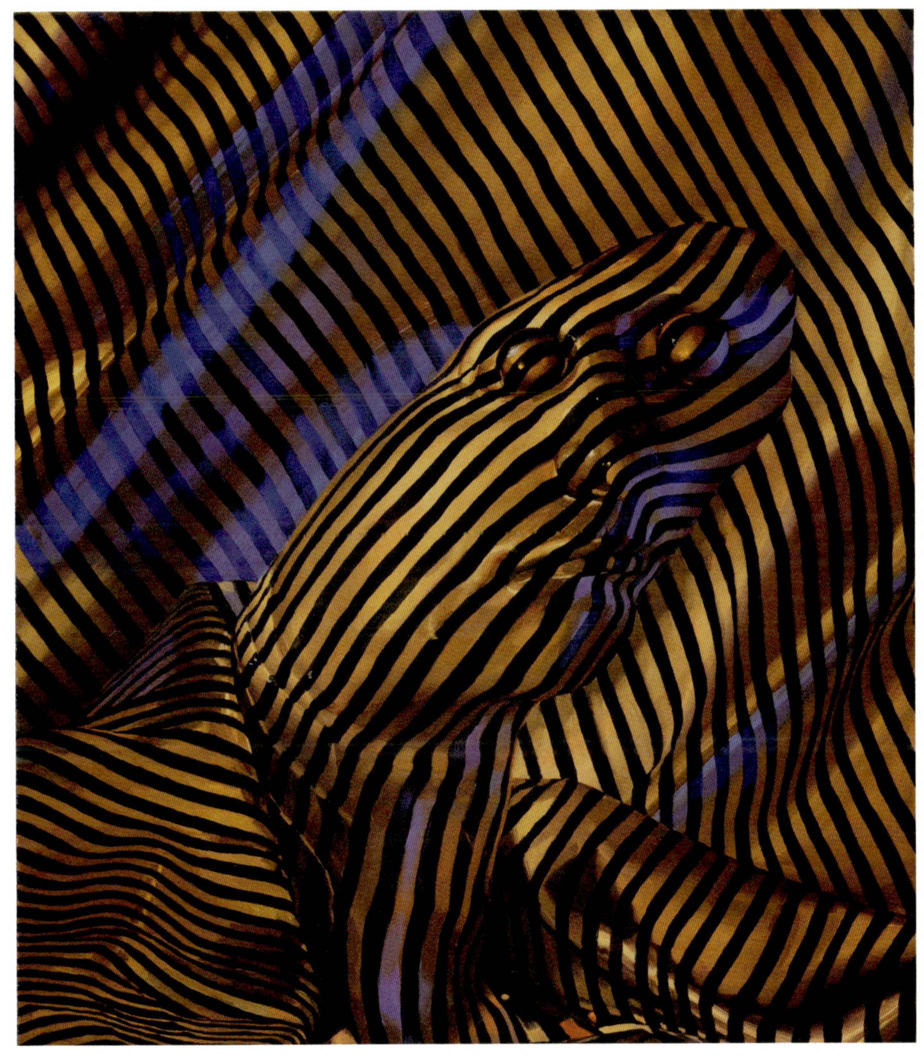

Untitled, 2011

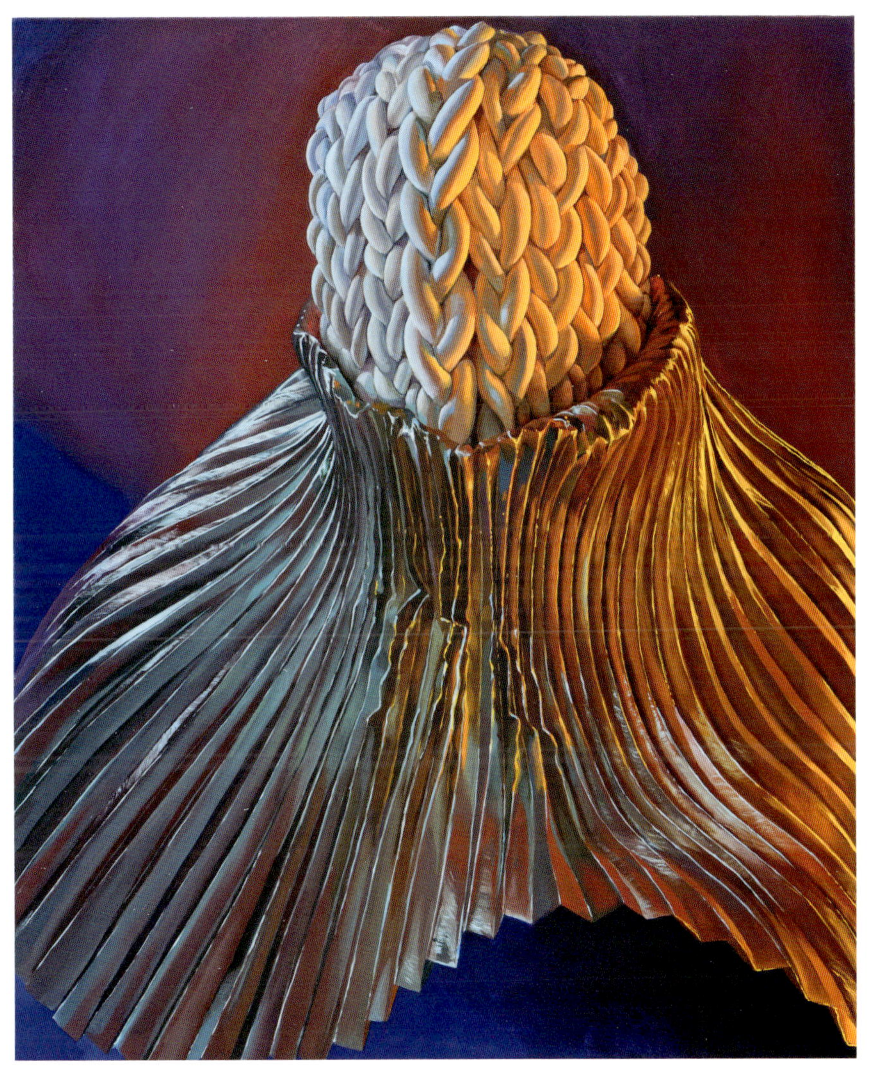

Collared, 2011

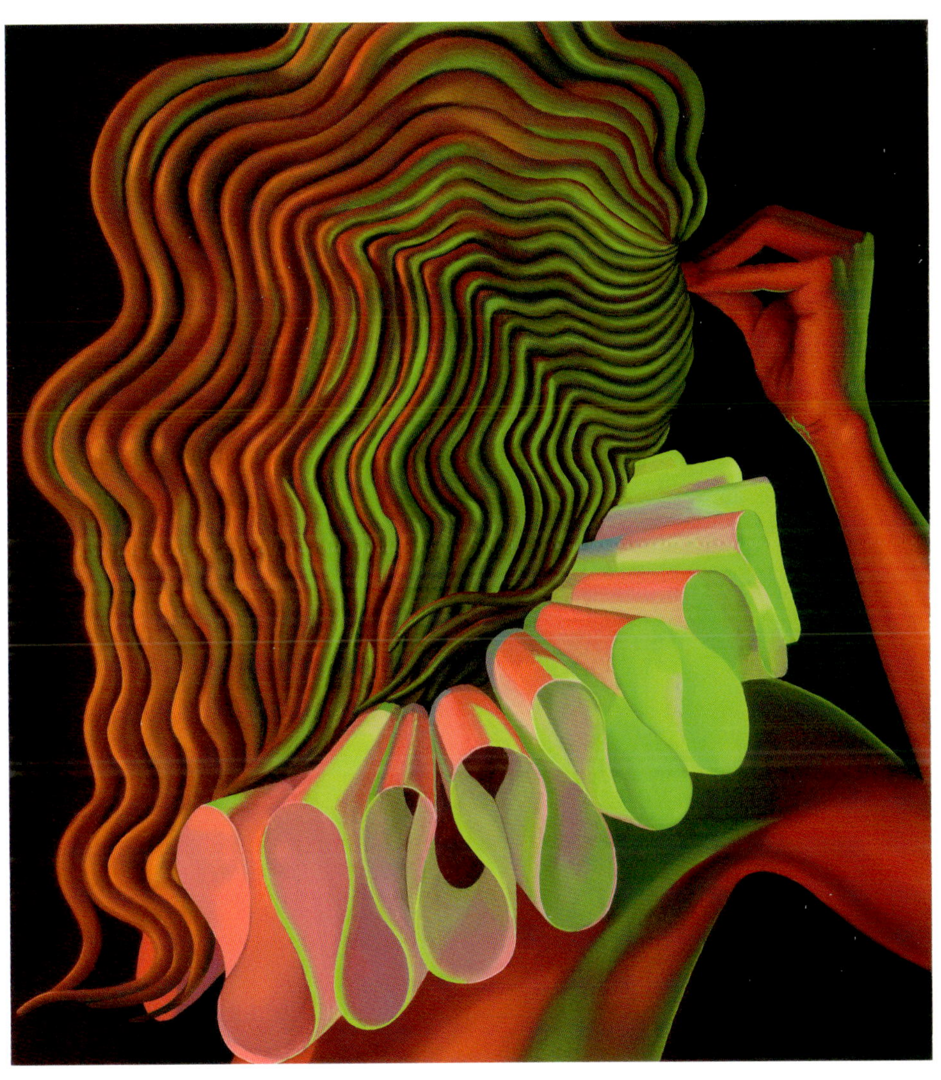

Bossy Pins, 2012

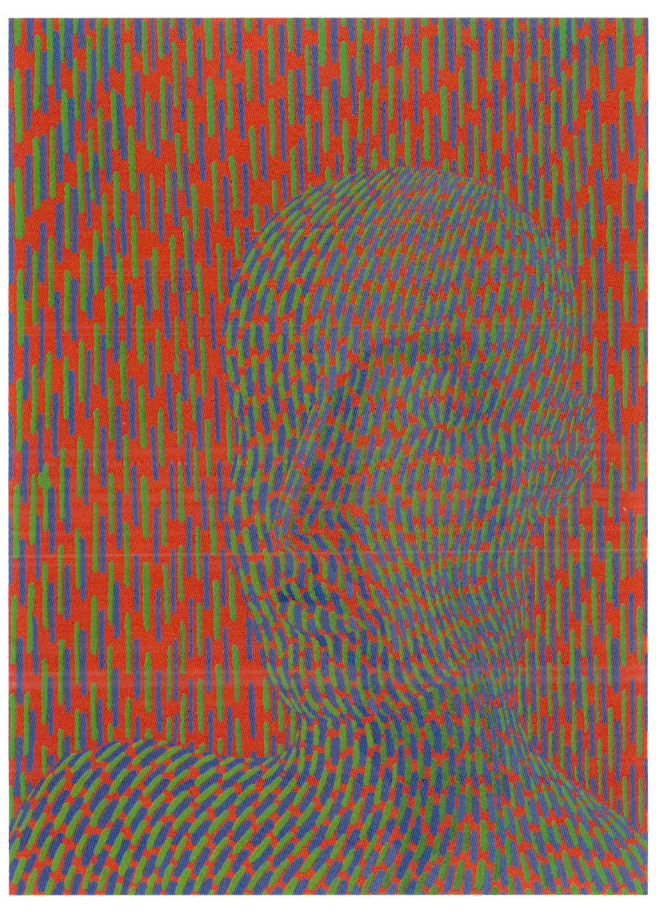

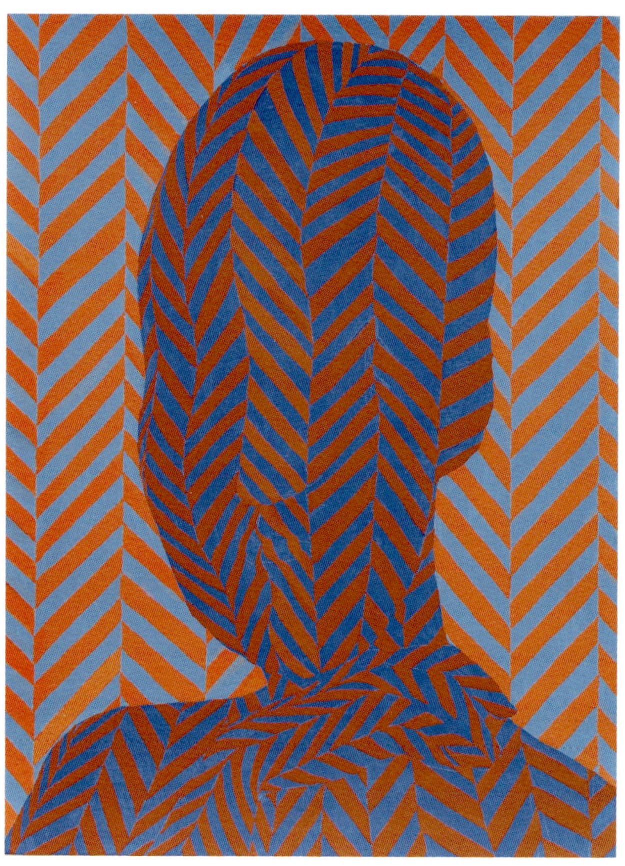

    Herringbone, 2011

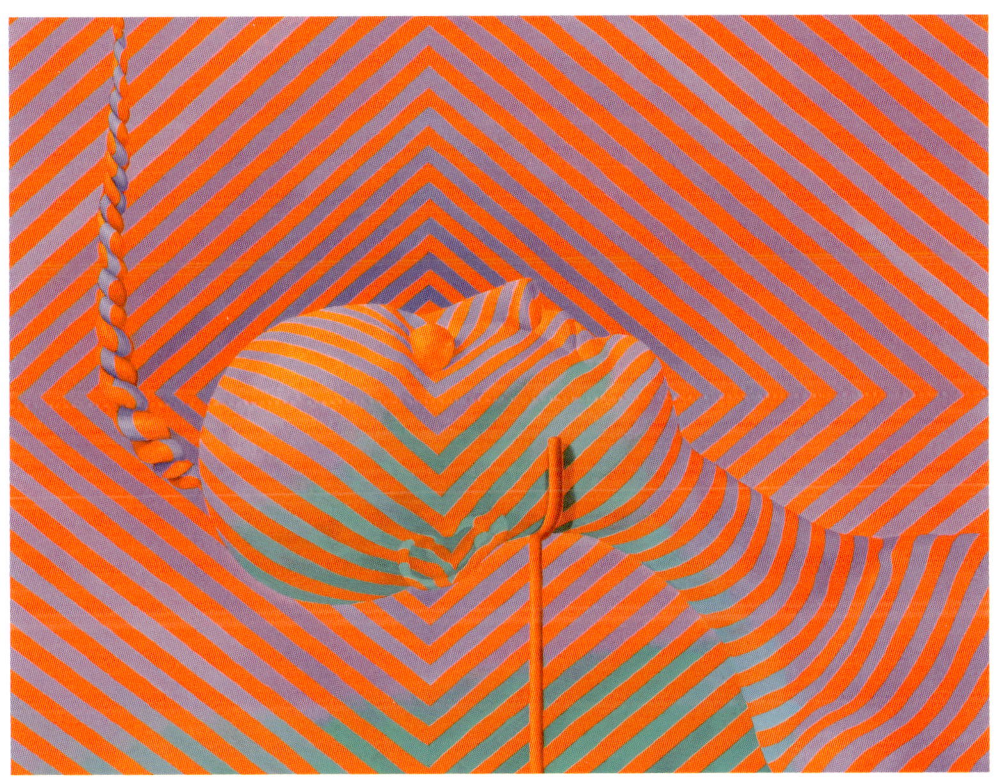

Prop, 2012

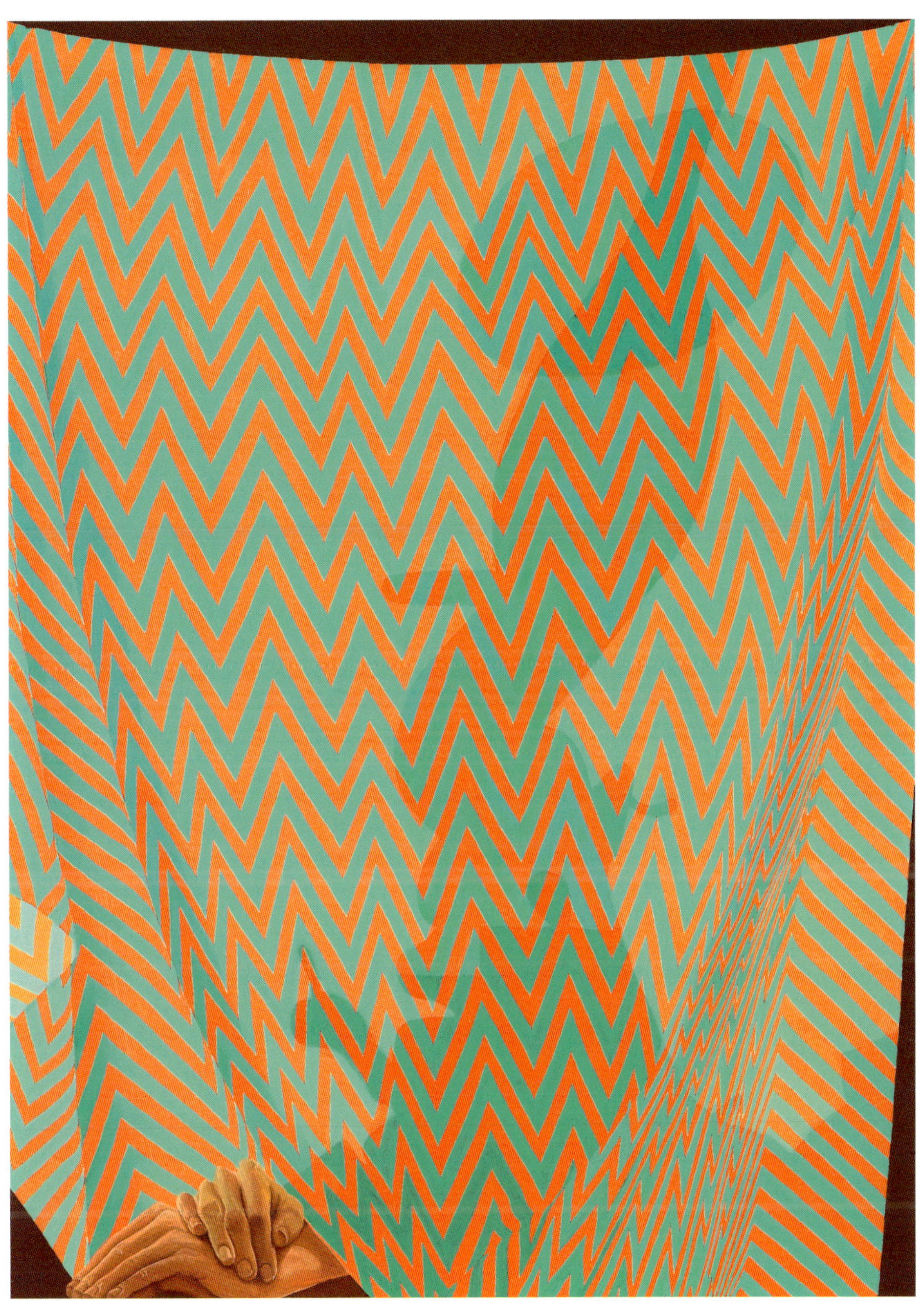

Strange Maine, 2012

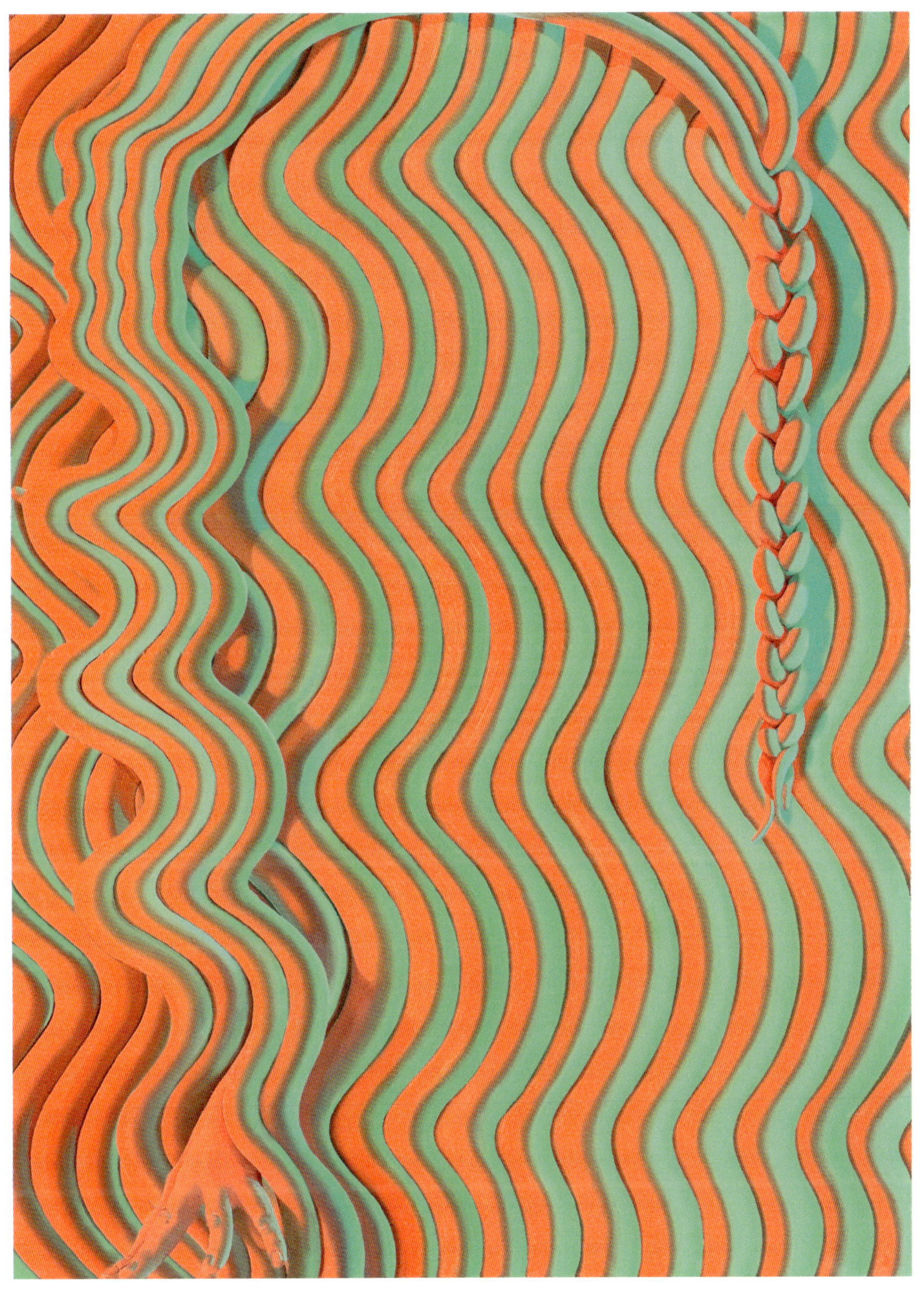

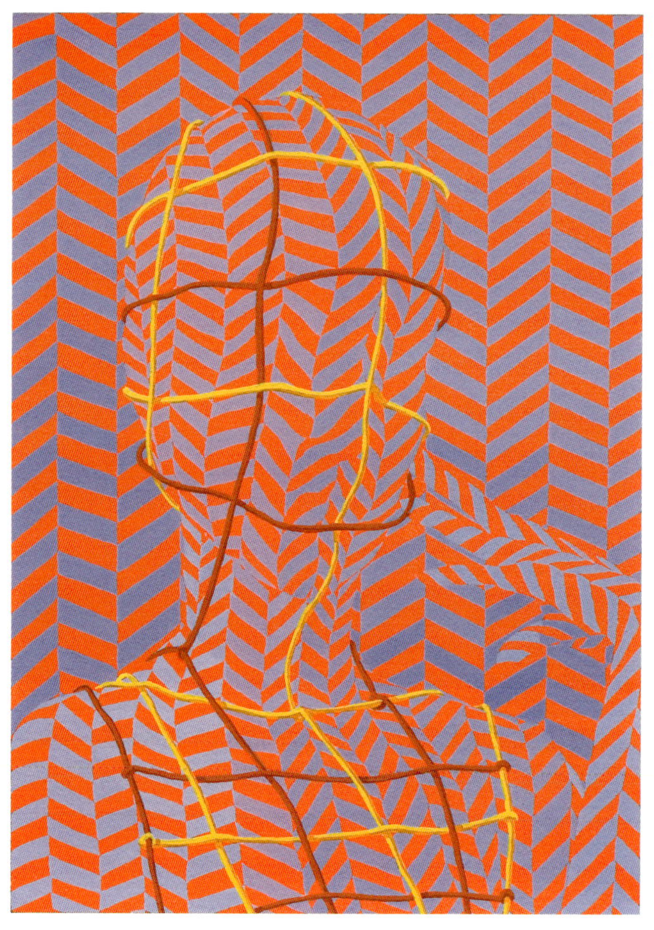

     Nets, 2012

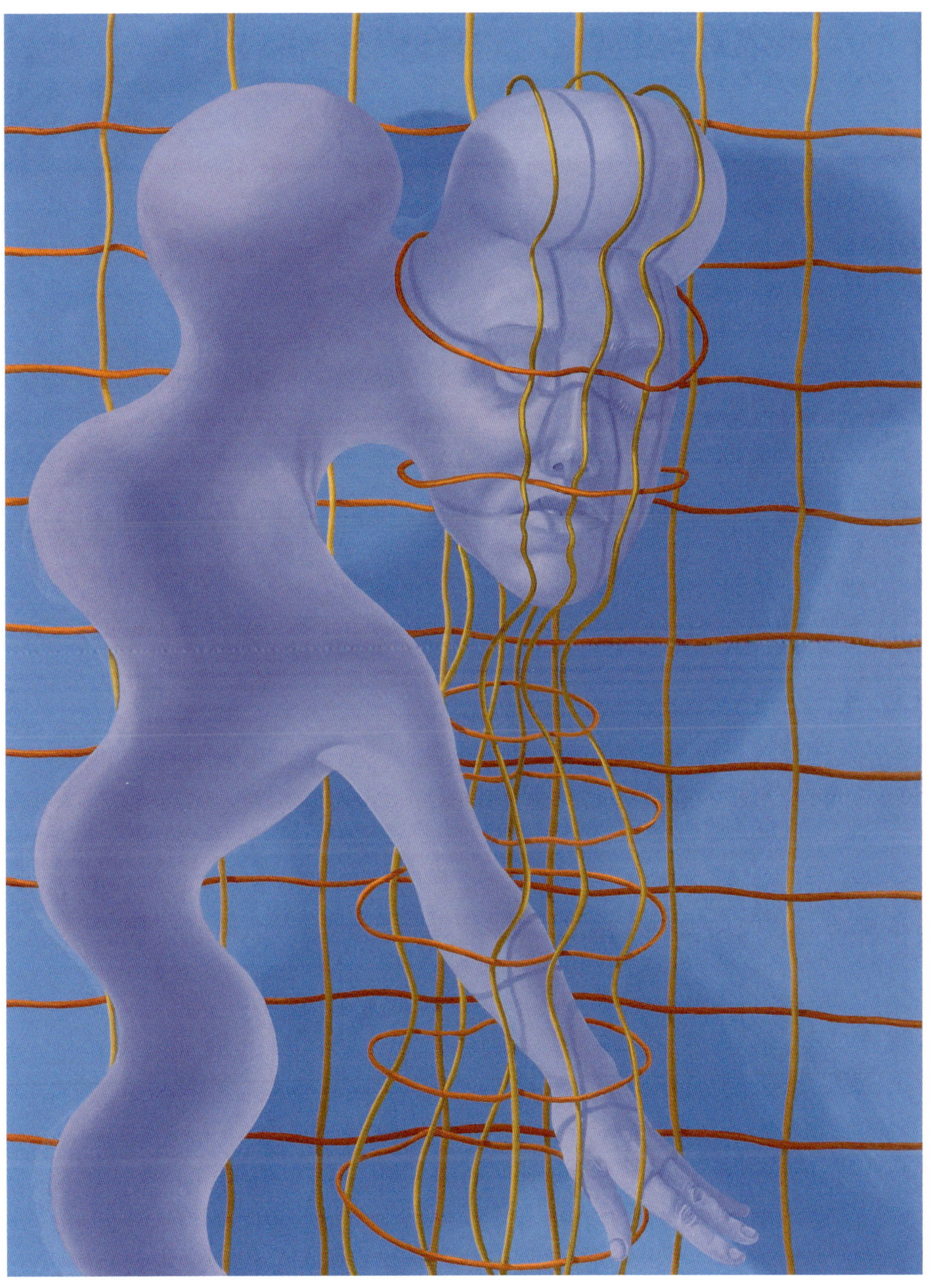

Blue Loomer, 2013

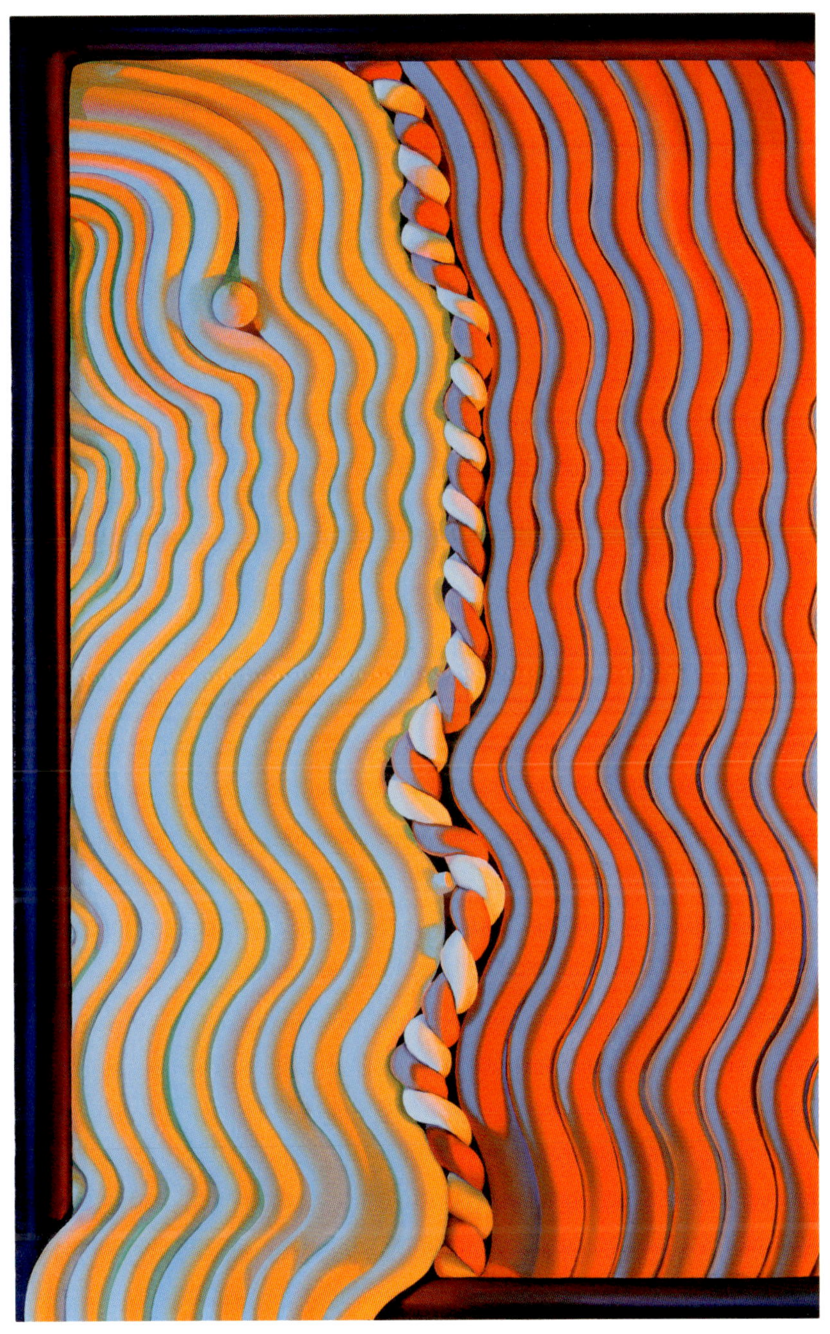

Rolling Shutter 2, 2013

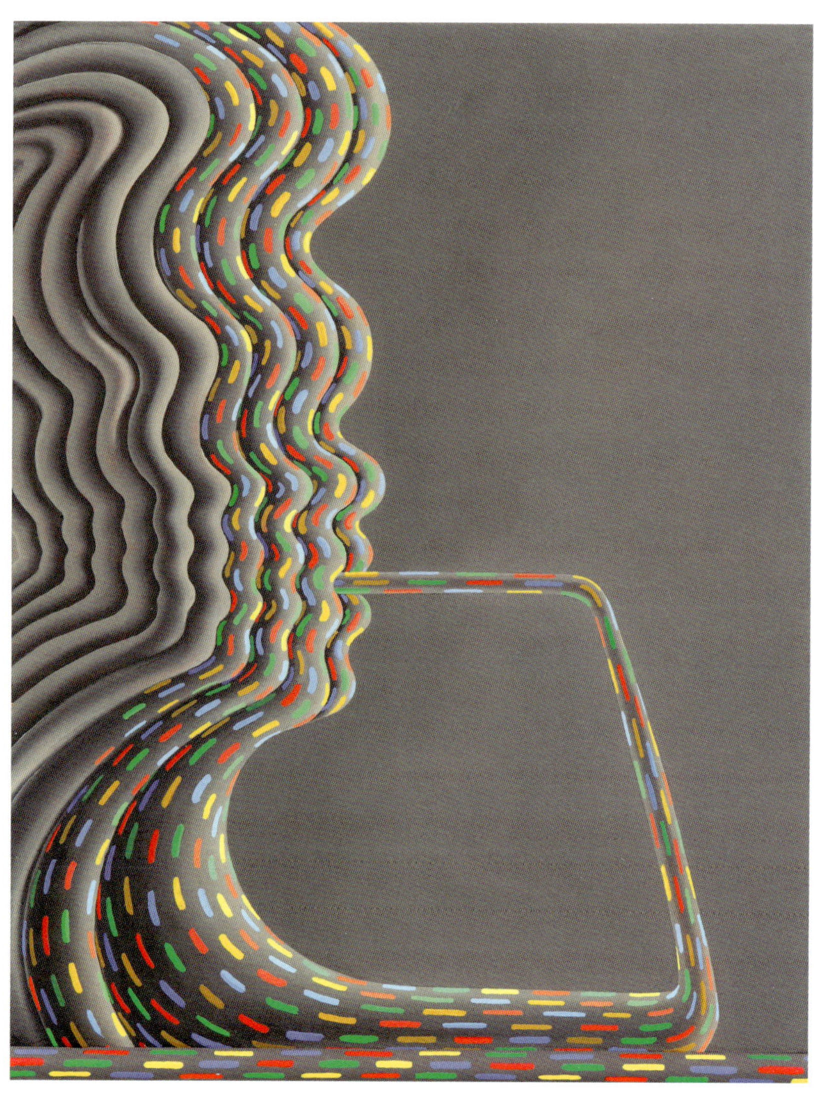

    Bottom Feeder, 2015

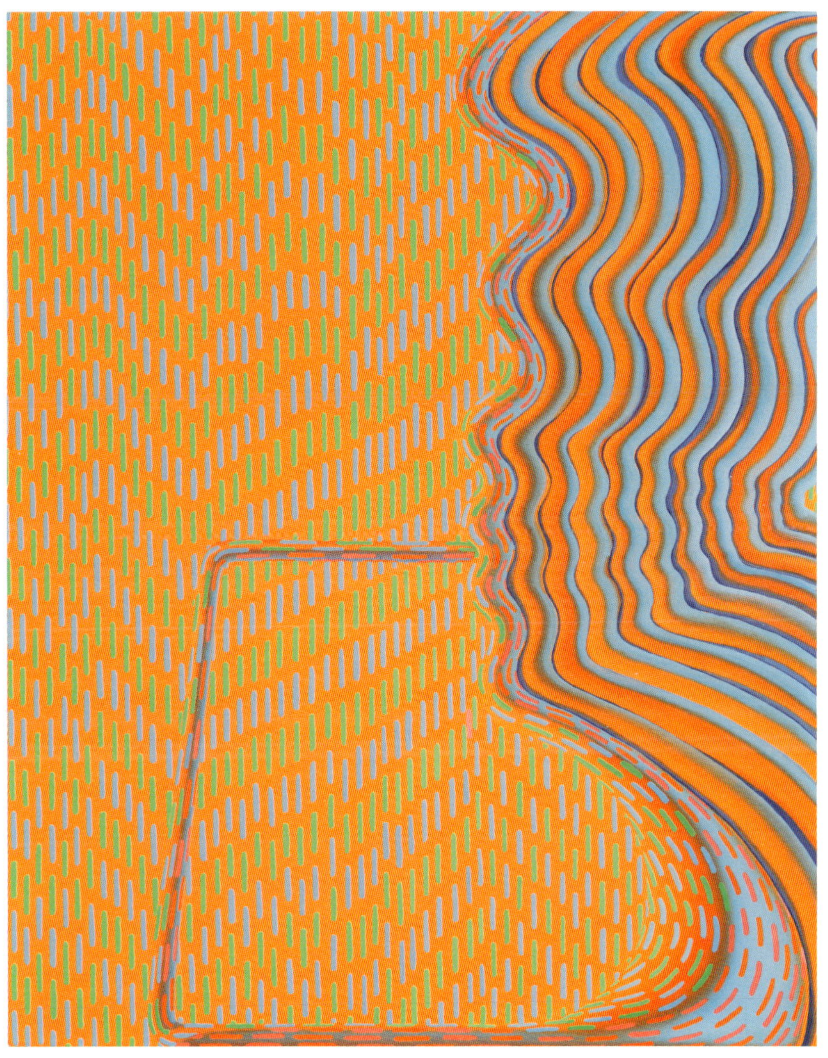

Orange Sucker, 2014

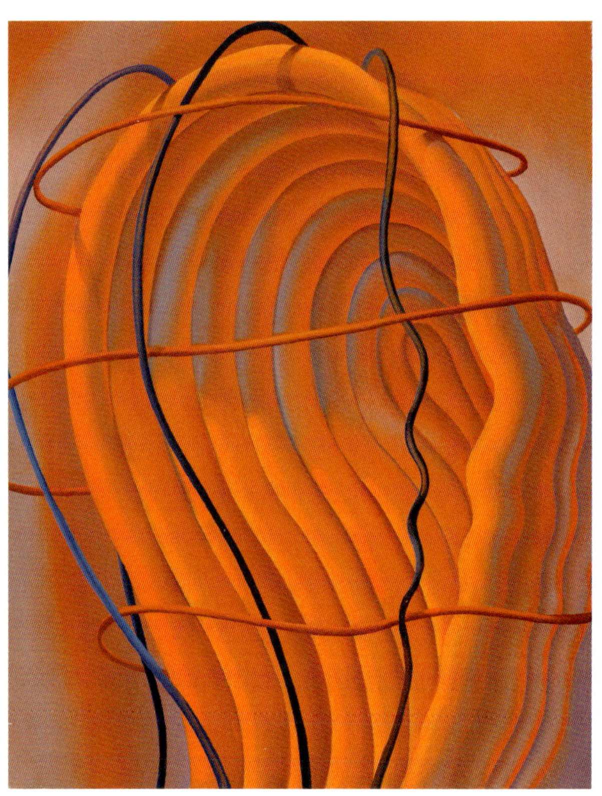

    Veined, Cuffed, Brained 1, 2013

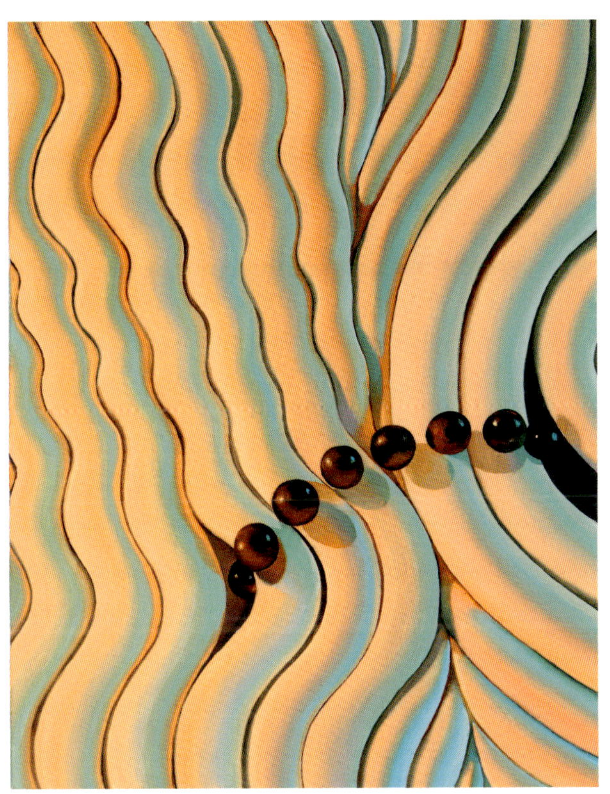

Veined, Cuffed, Brained 2, 2013

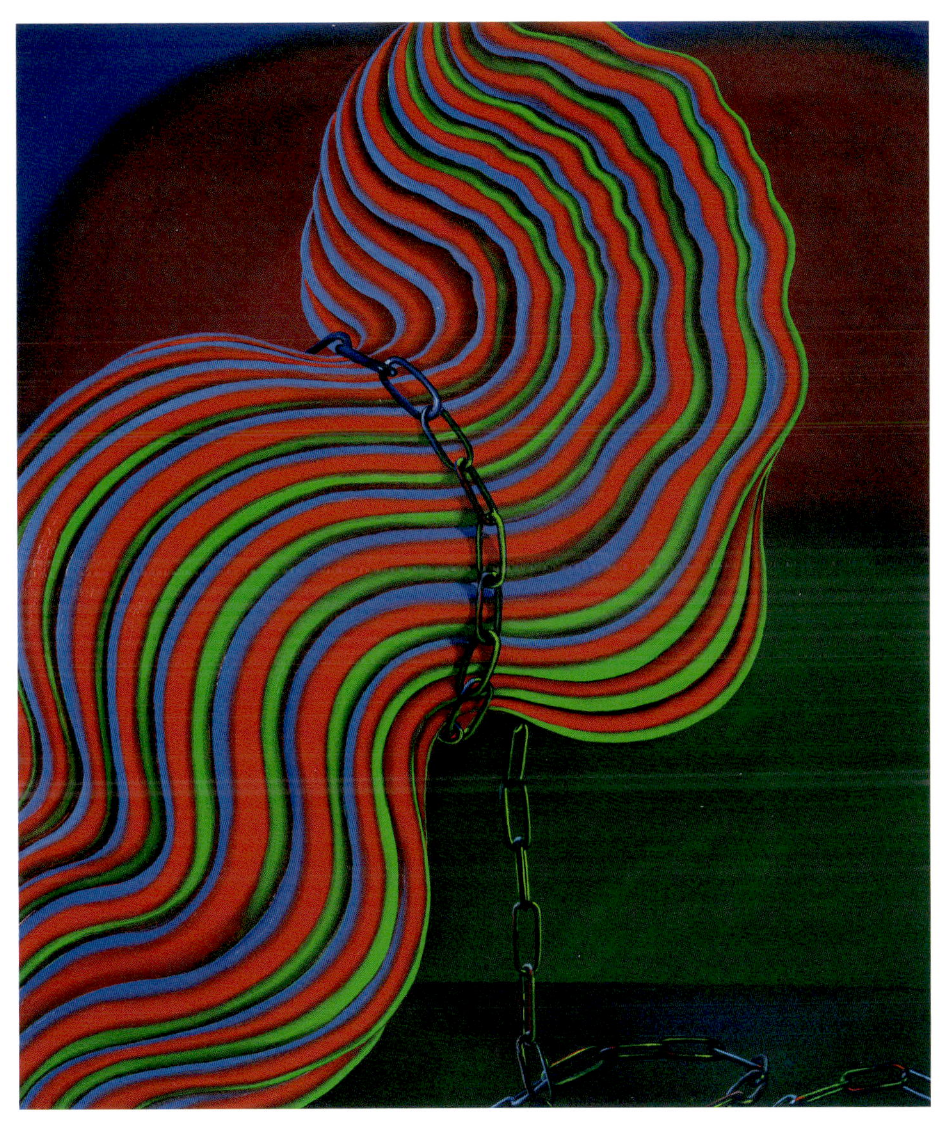

Bridle, 2013

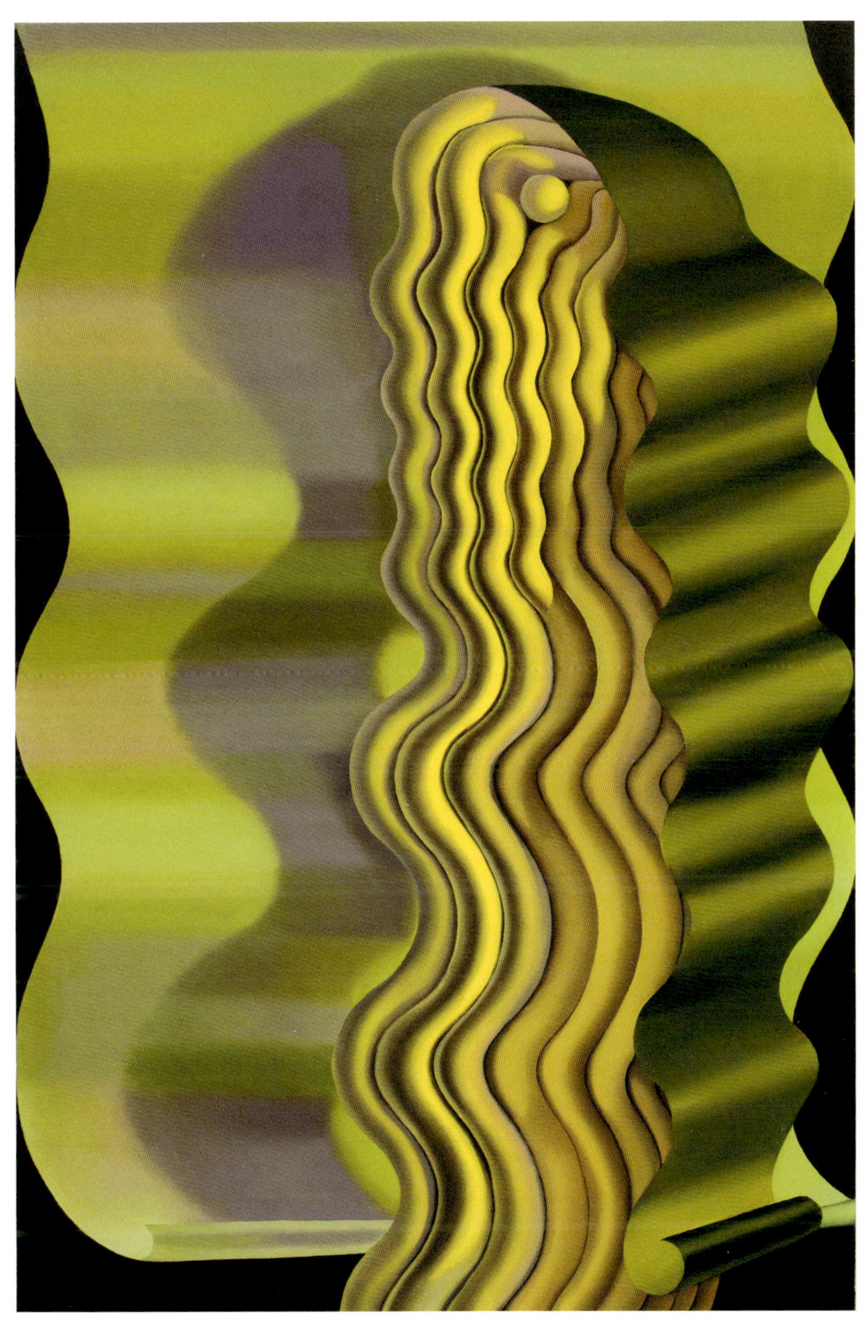

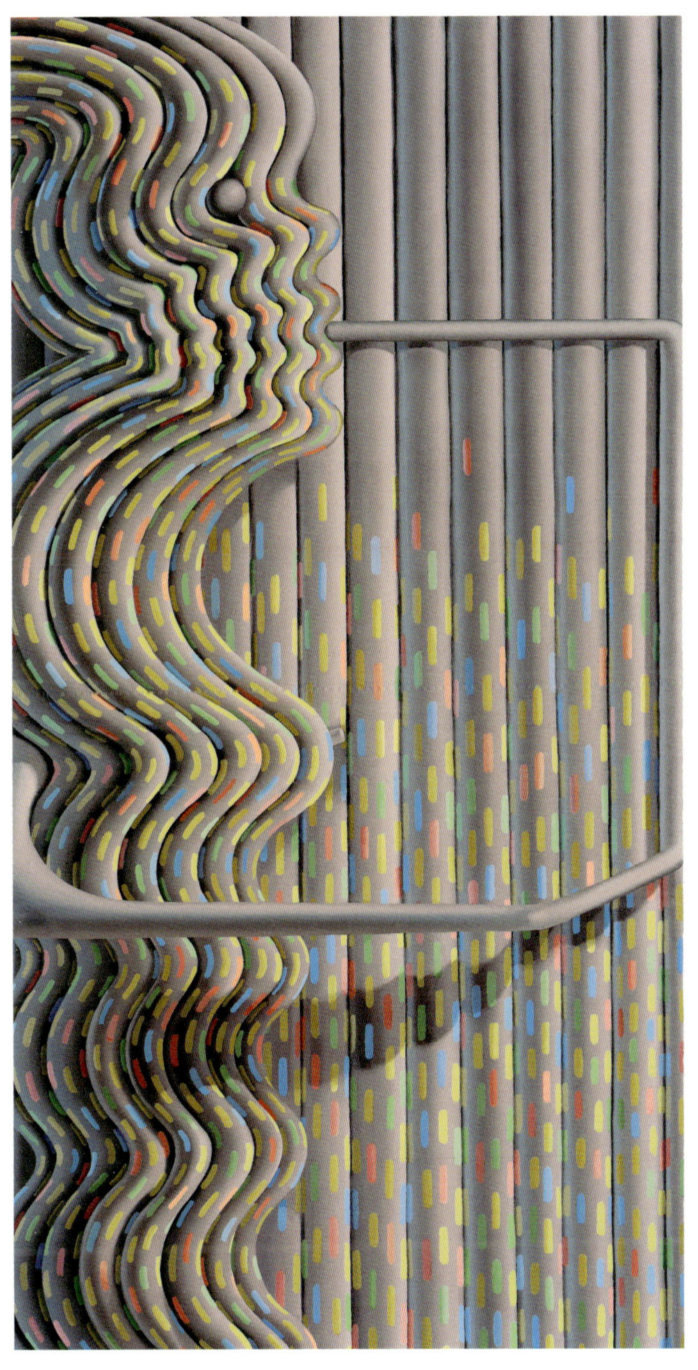

Feeder, 2014

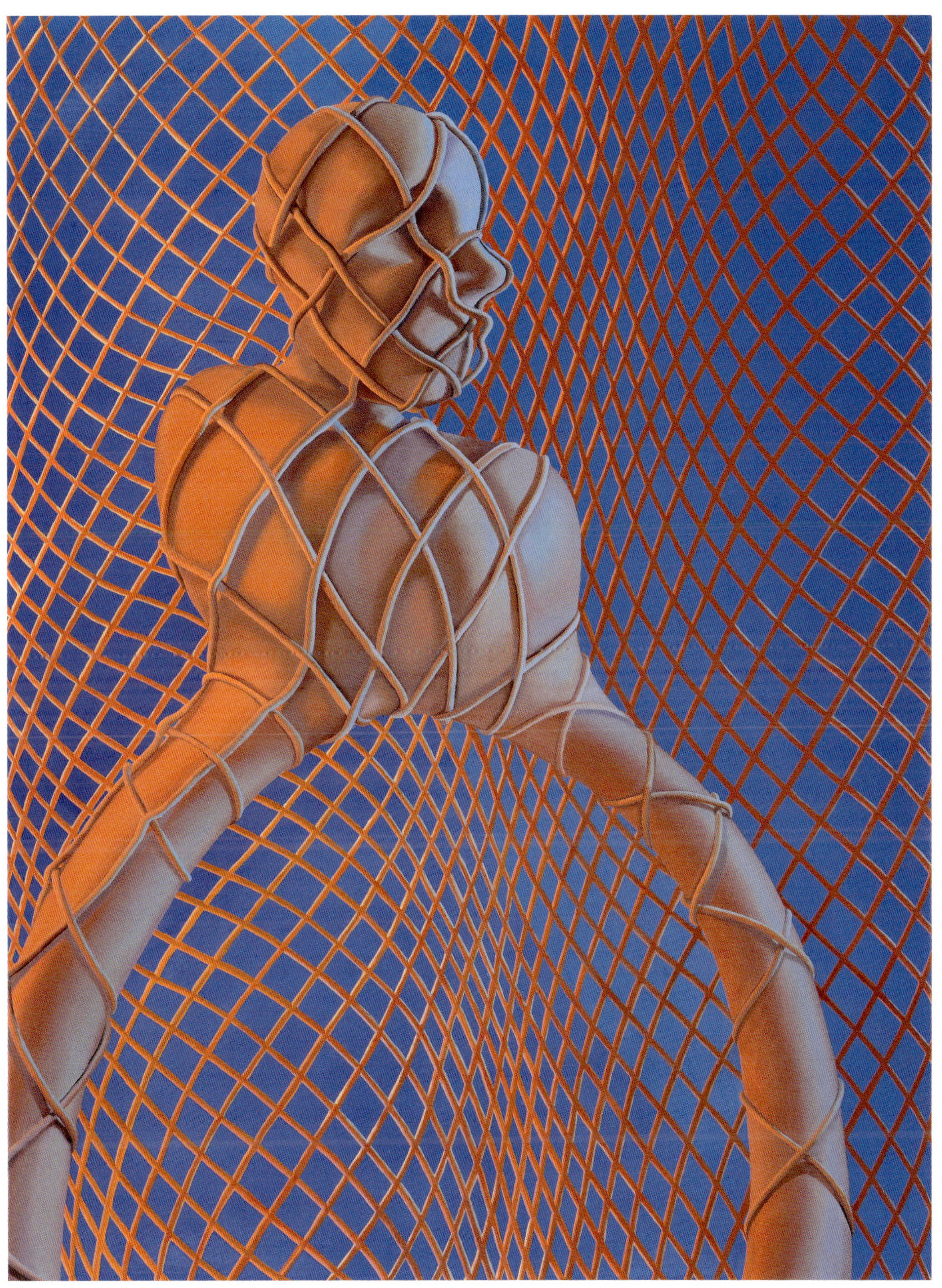

Strider 2, 2014

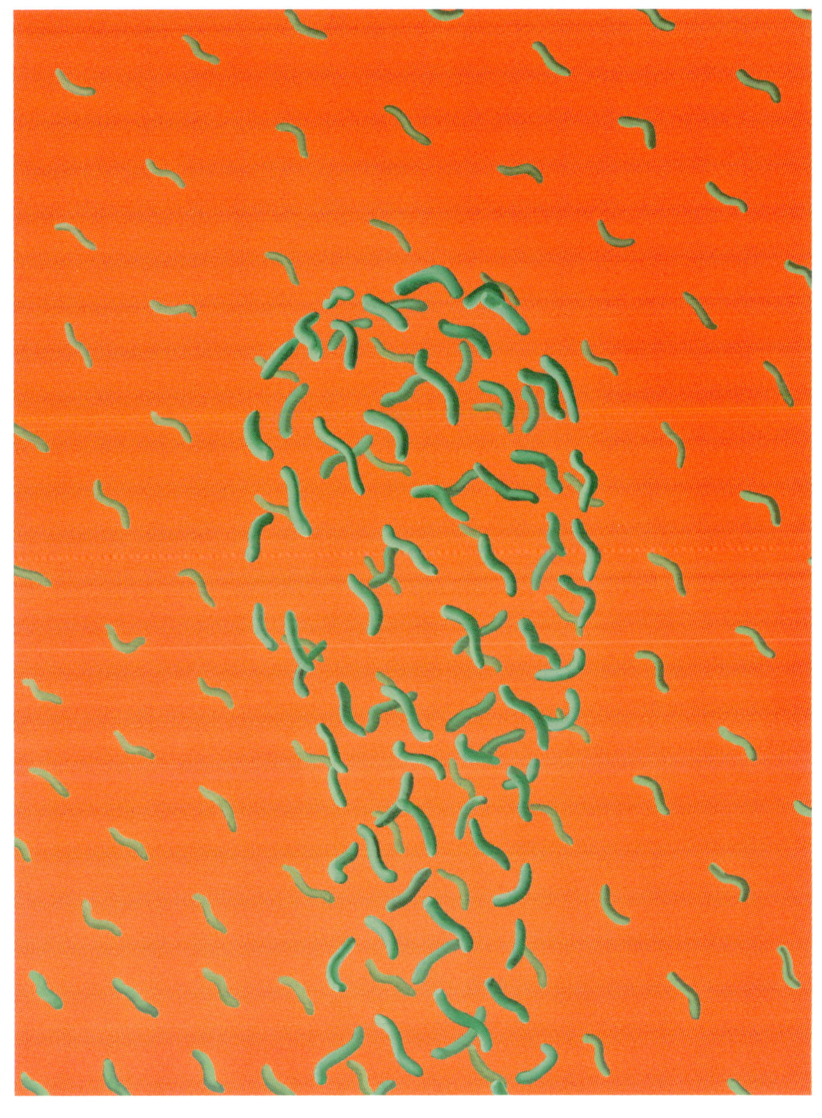

Squirm, 2014

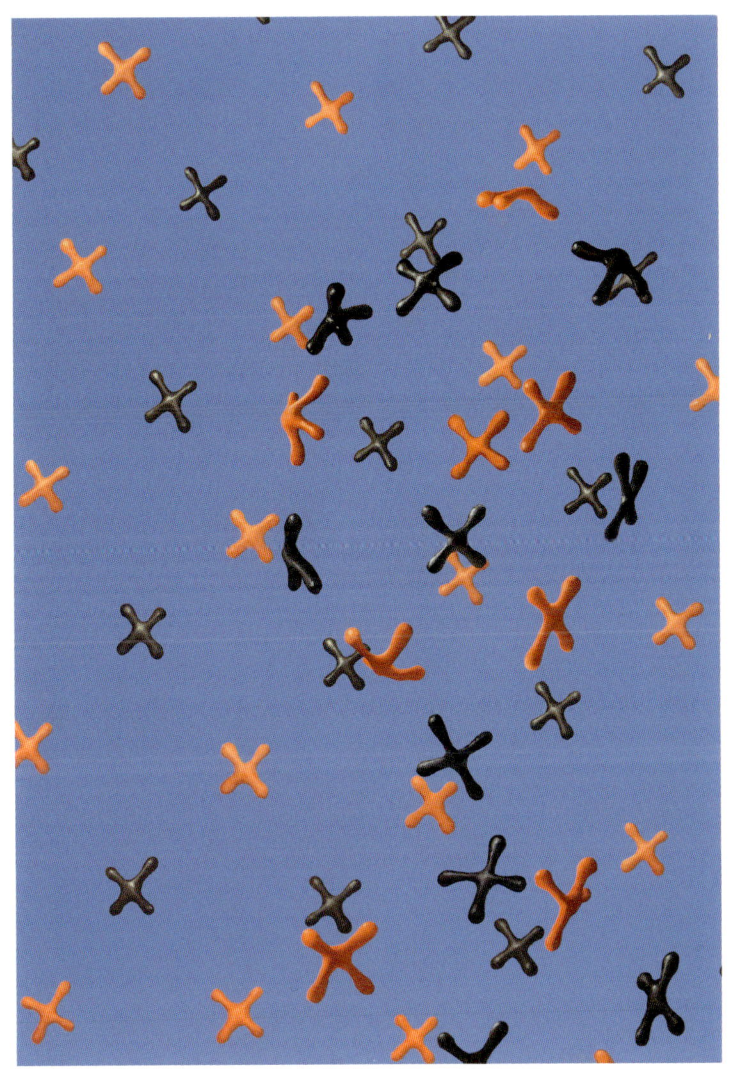

Motes, 2015

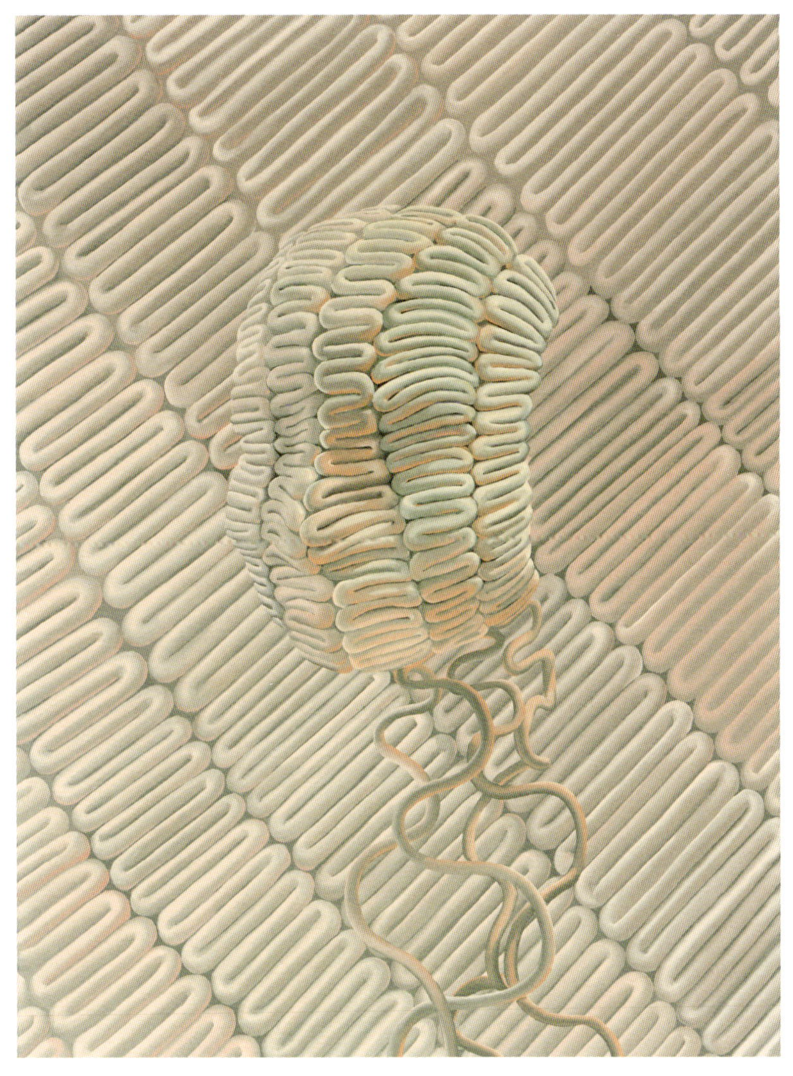

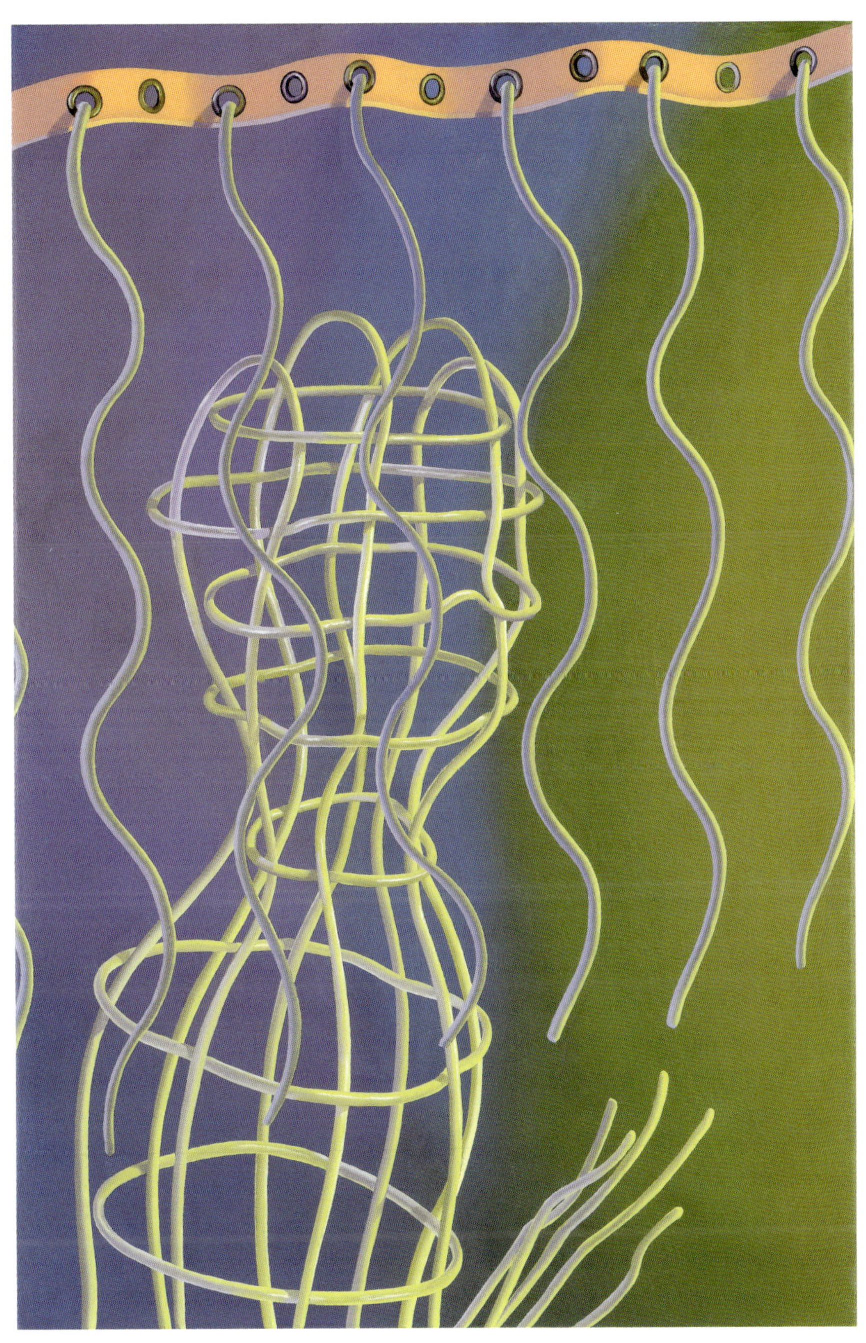

Valance, 2014/2015

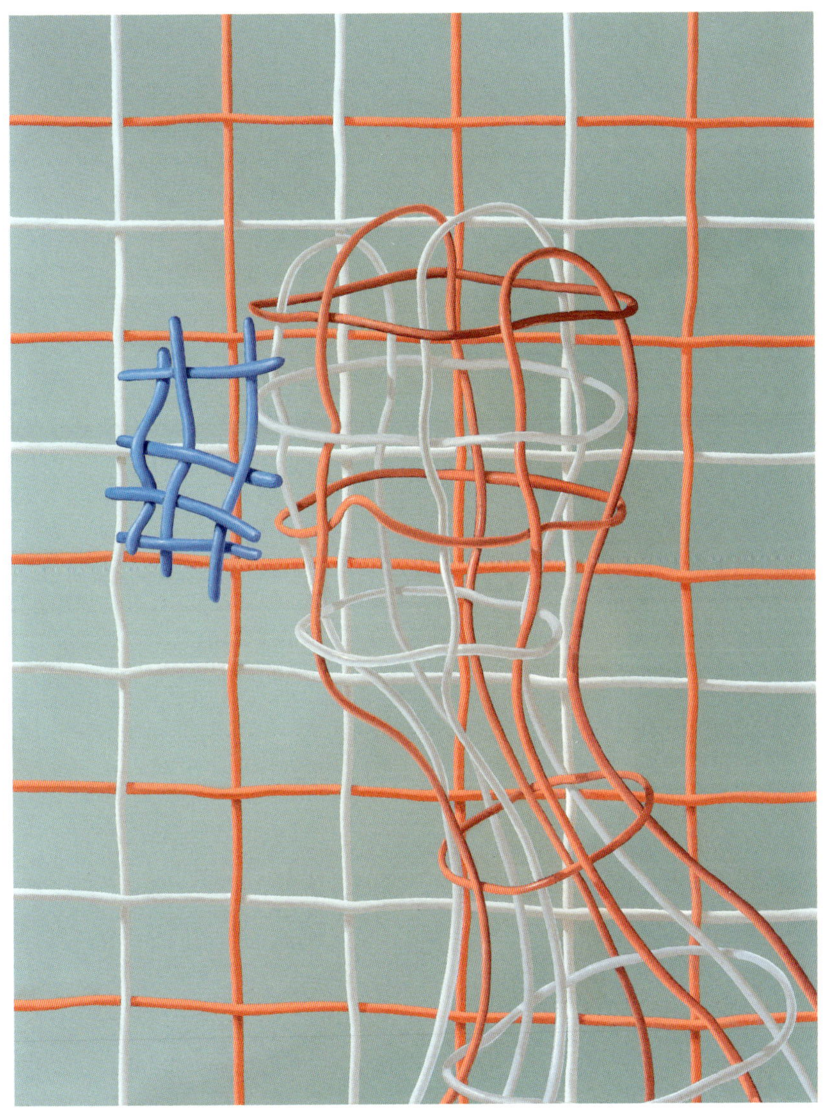

Monad, 2014

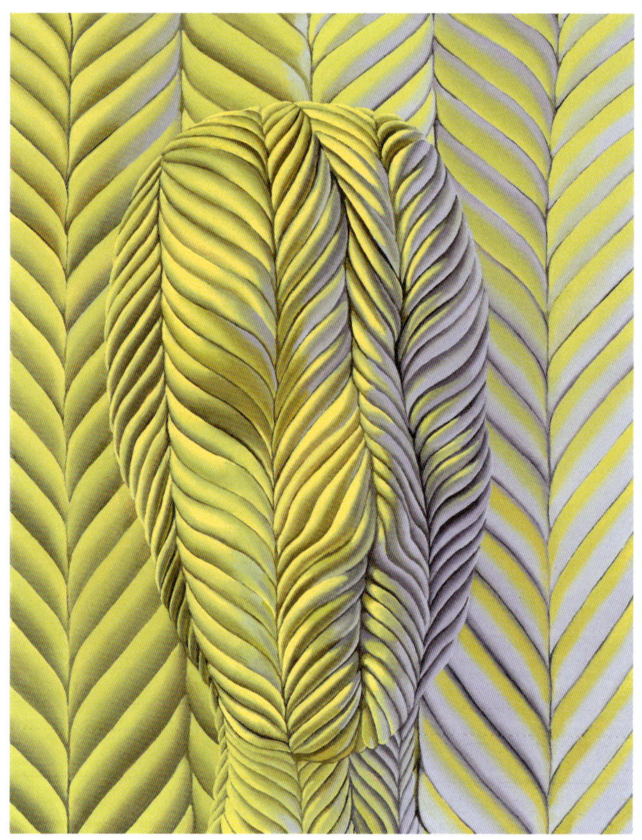

78   *Troll,* 2014

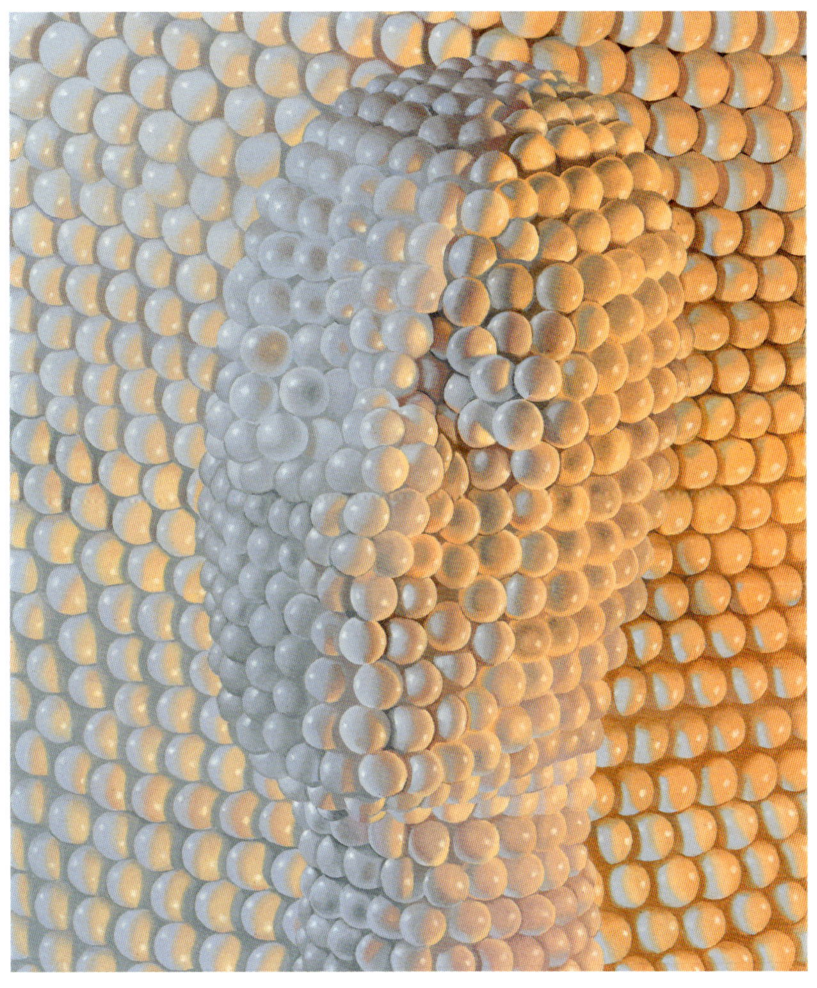

Saccades, 2014

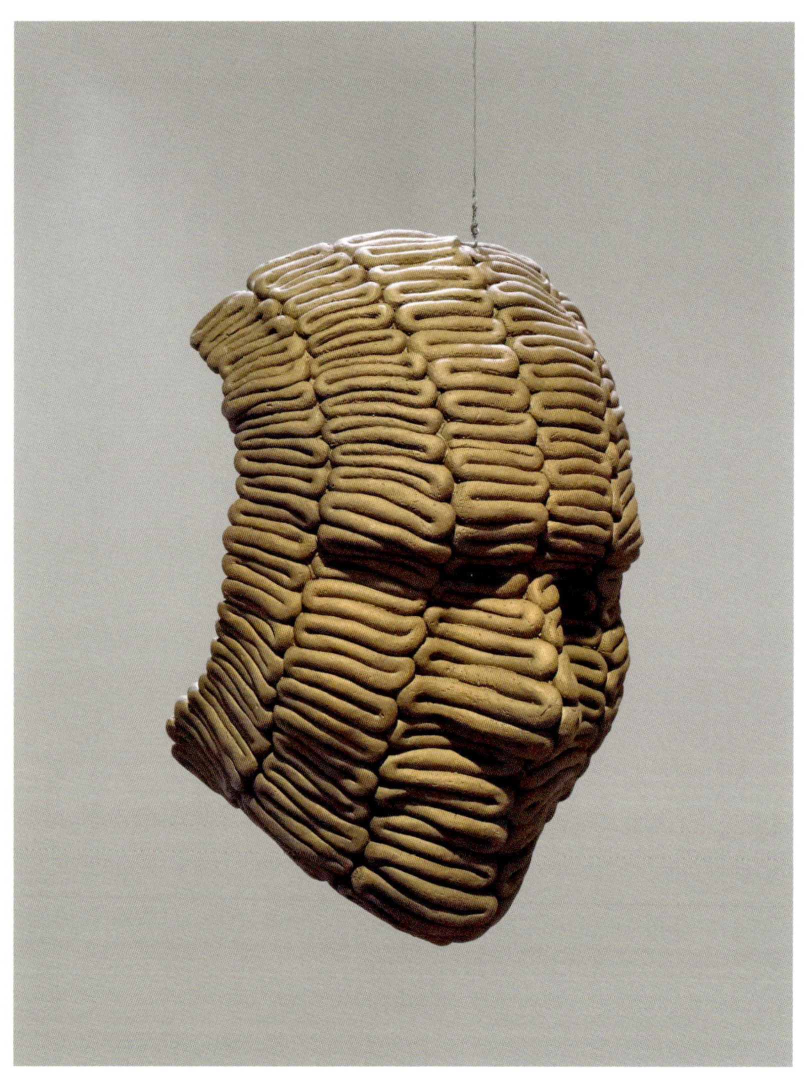

    Chur, 2014/15

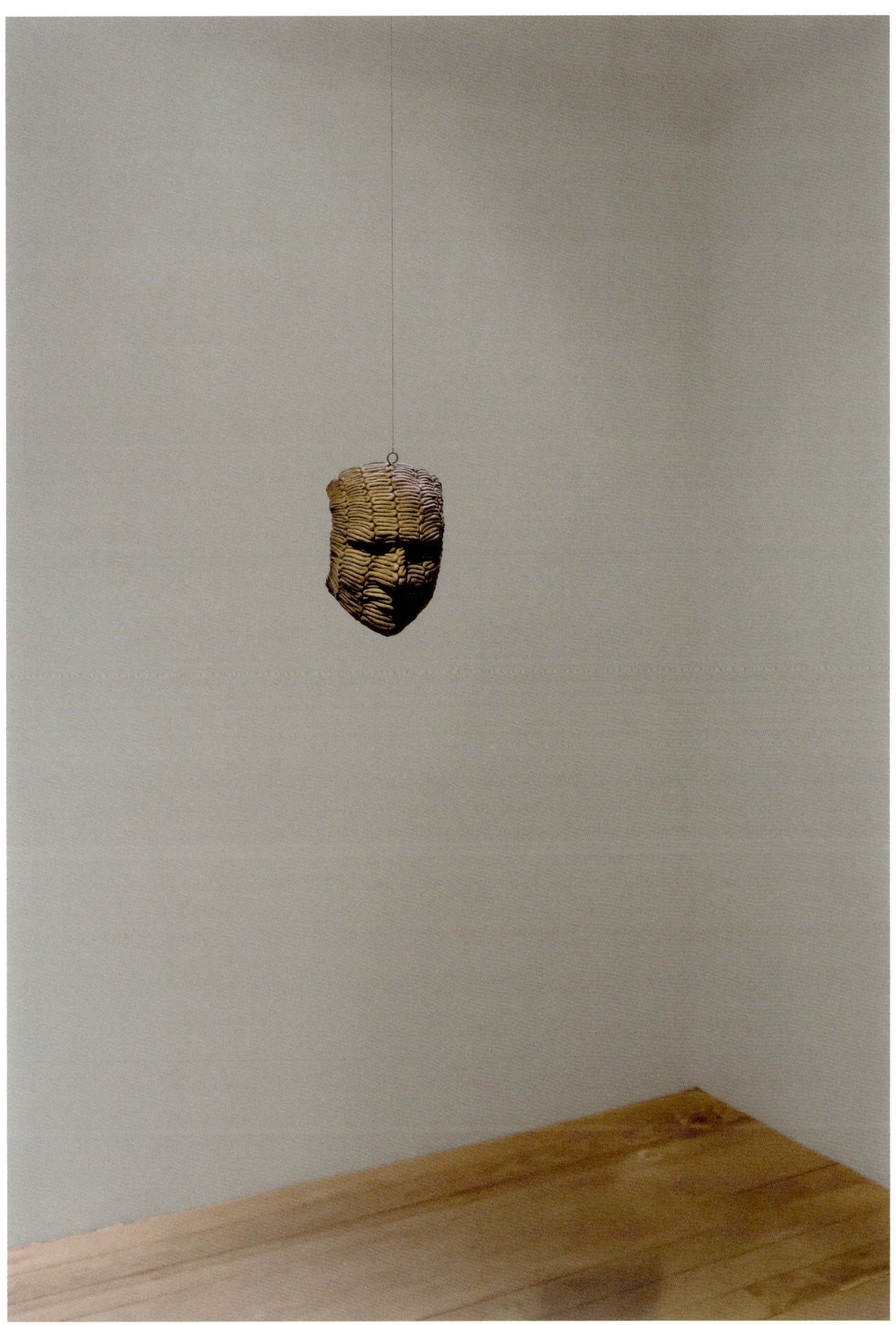

Installation view, Foxy Production, 2015

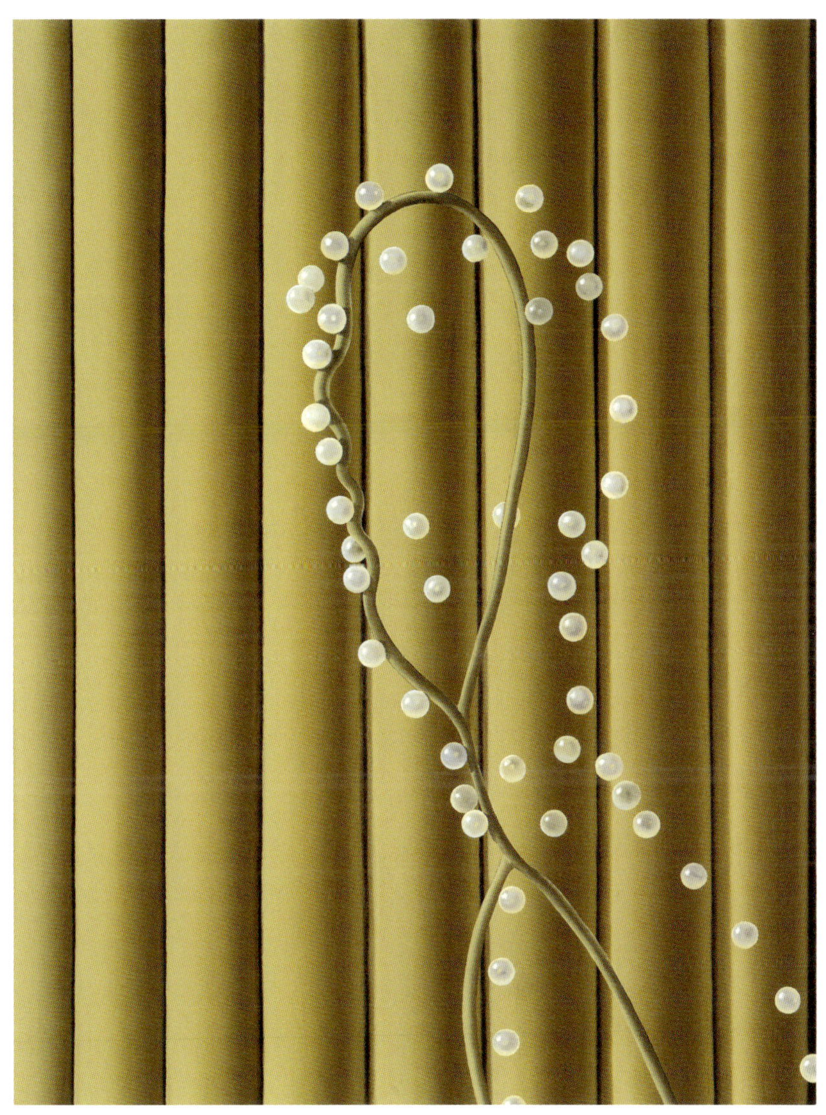

Marker, 2015

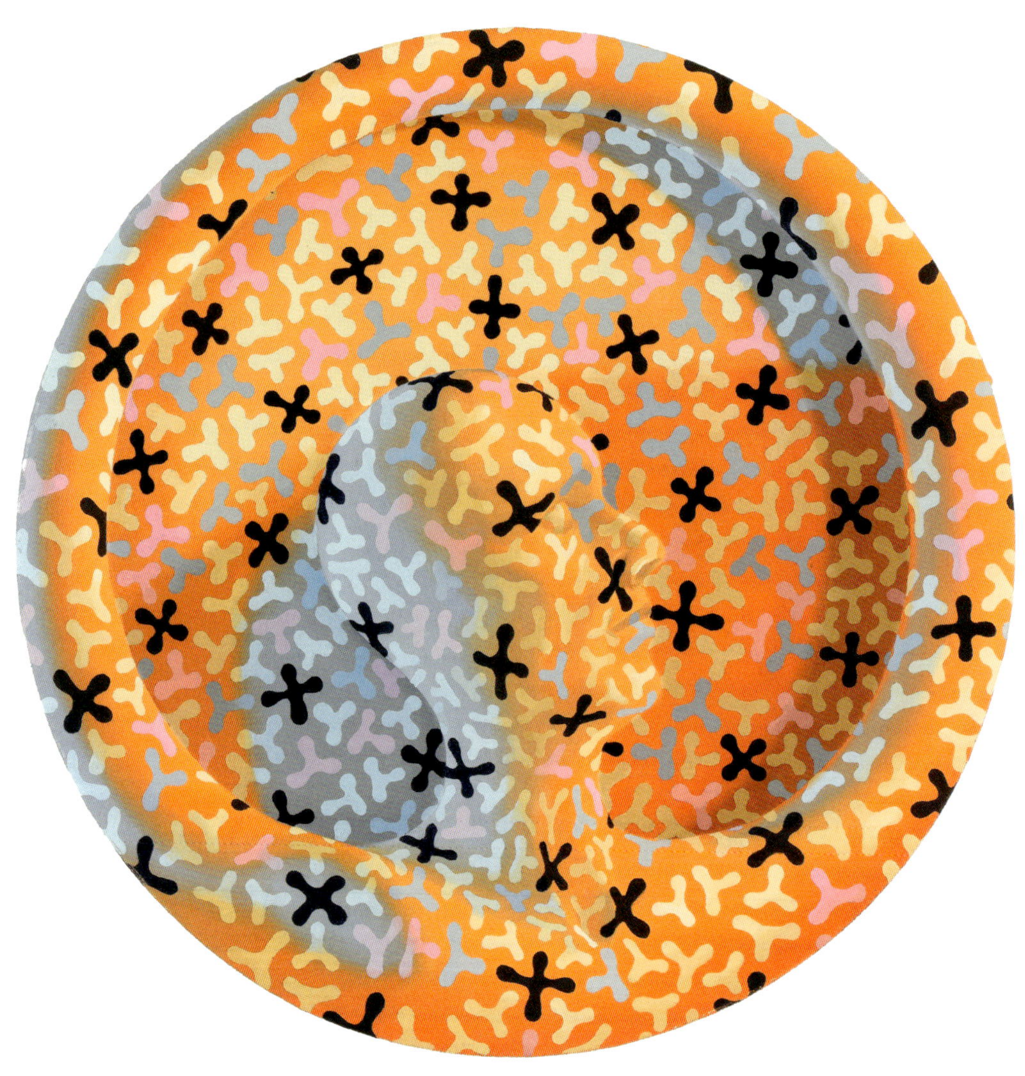

84   *Reef*, 2015

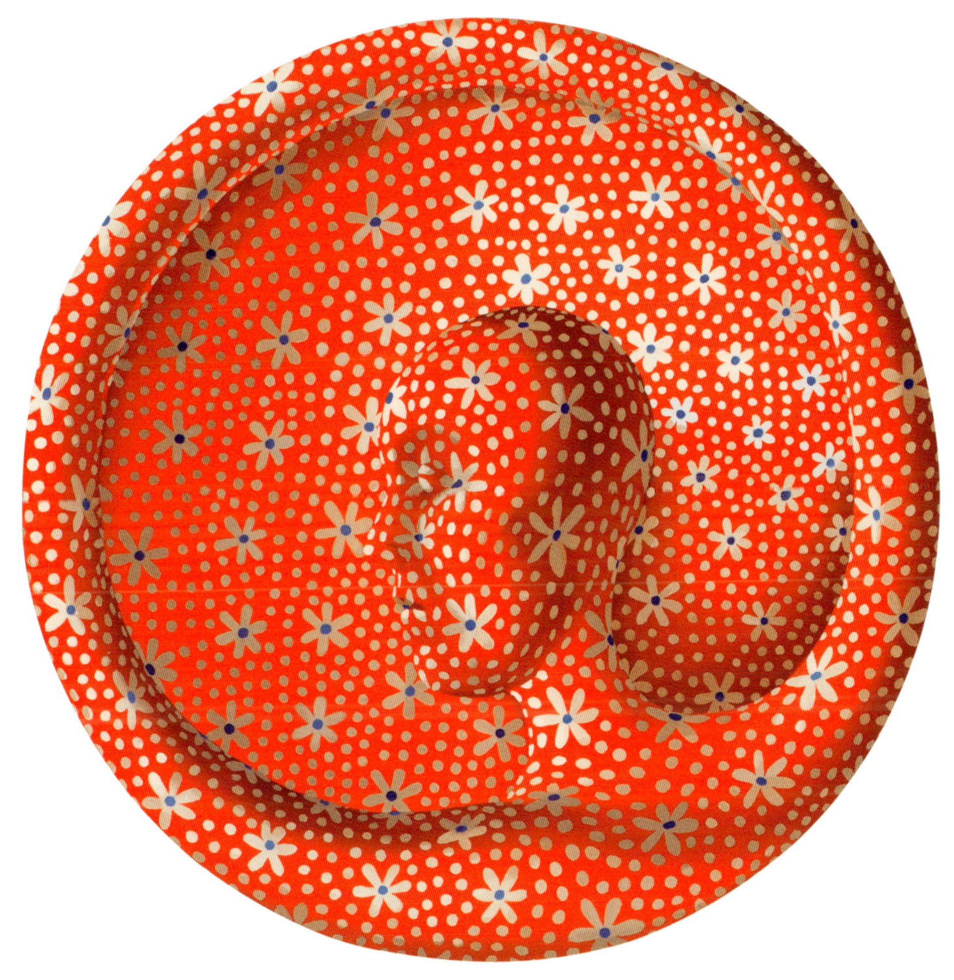

Field, 2014

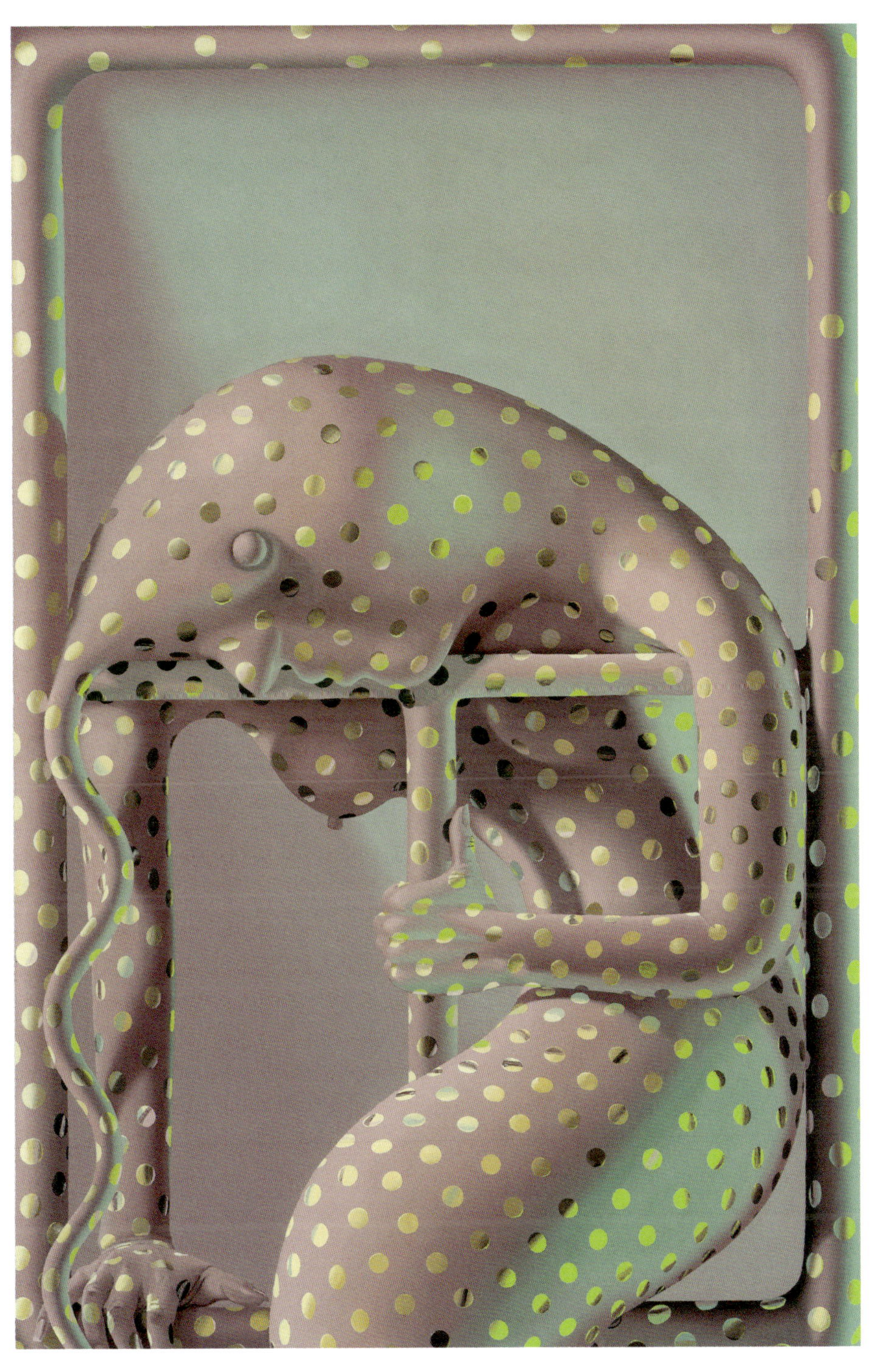

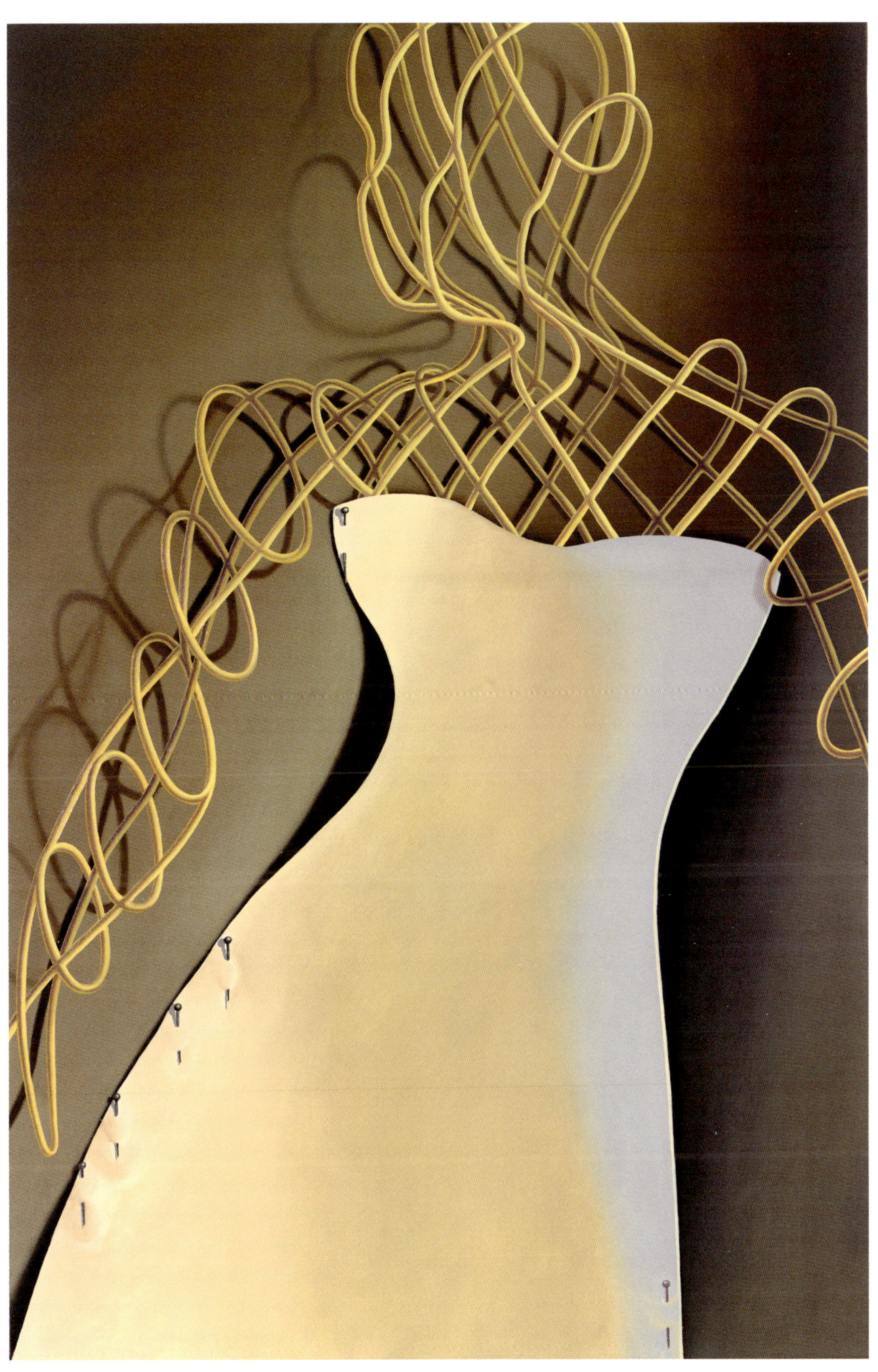

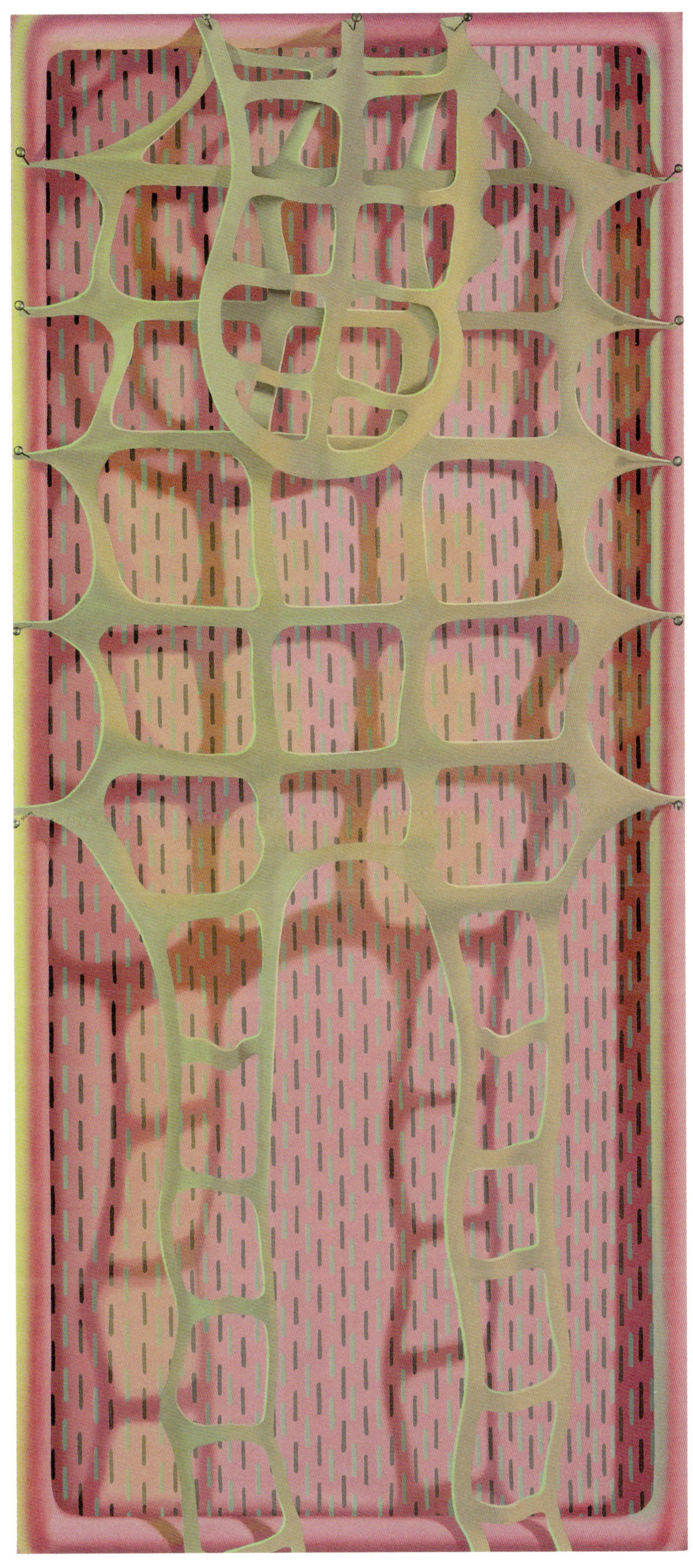

Hide, 2015

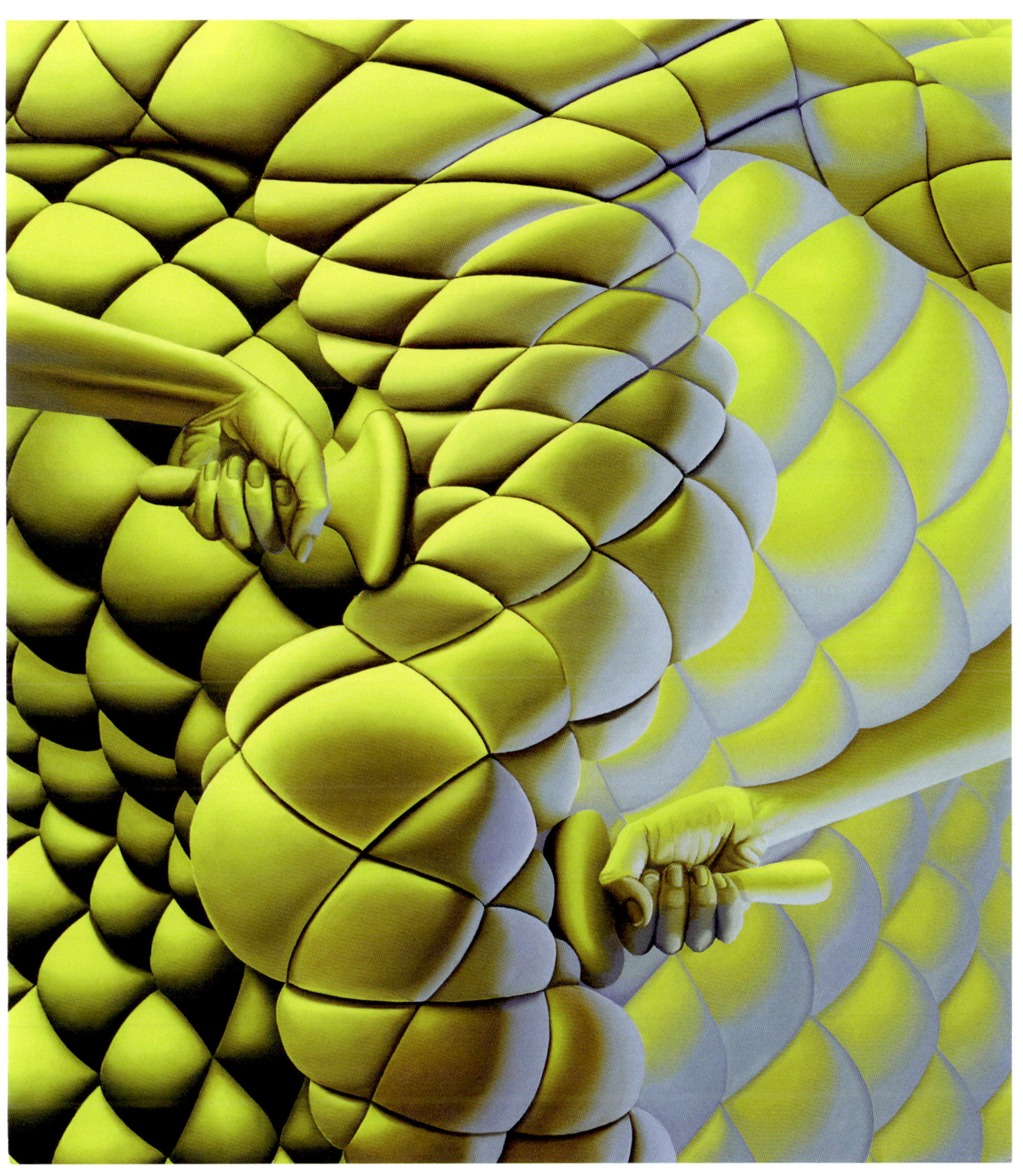

Warm Leatherette, 2015

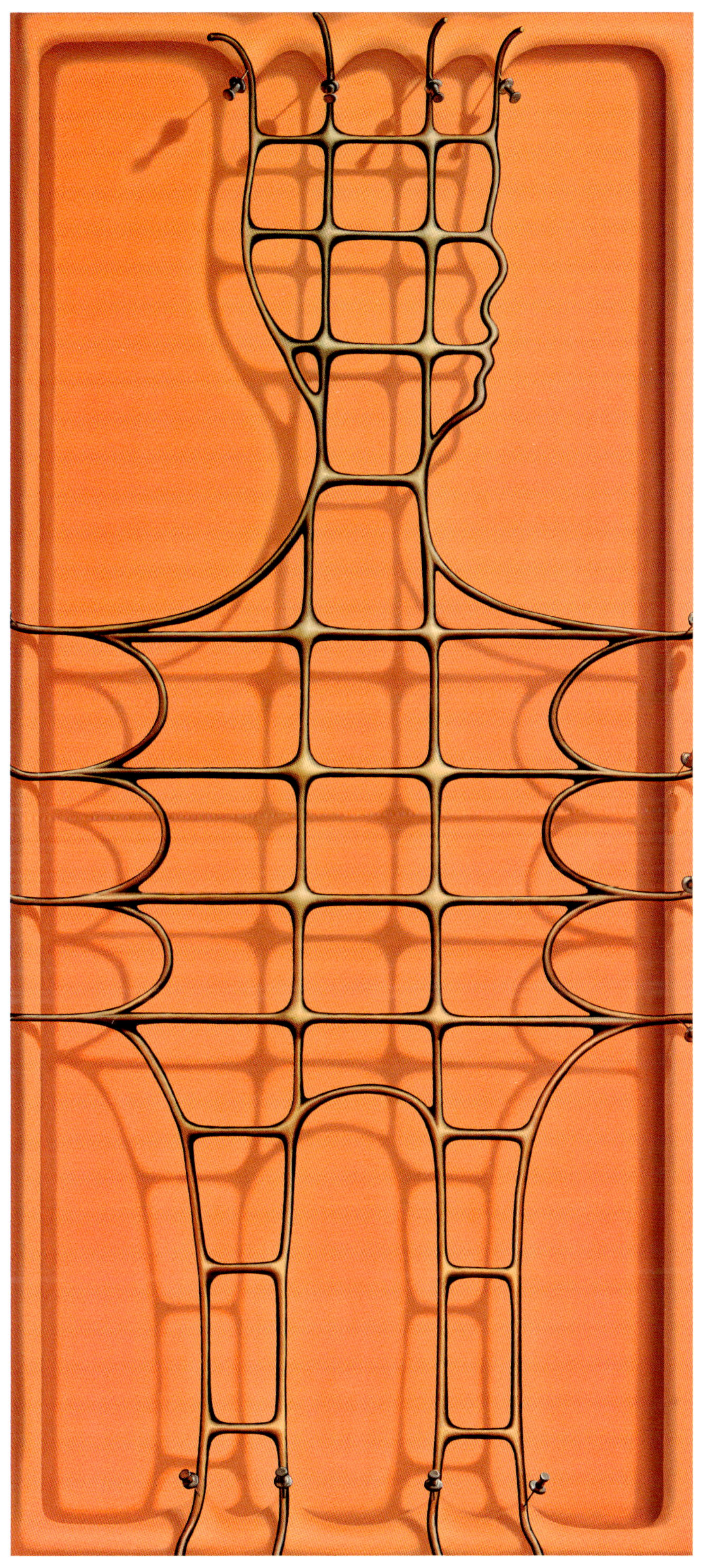

La Maitresse, 2015

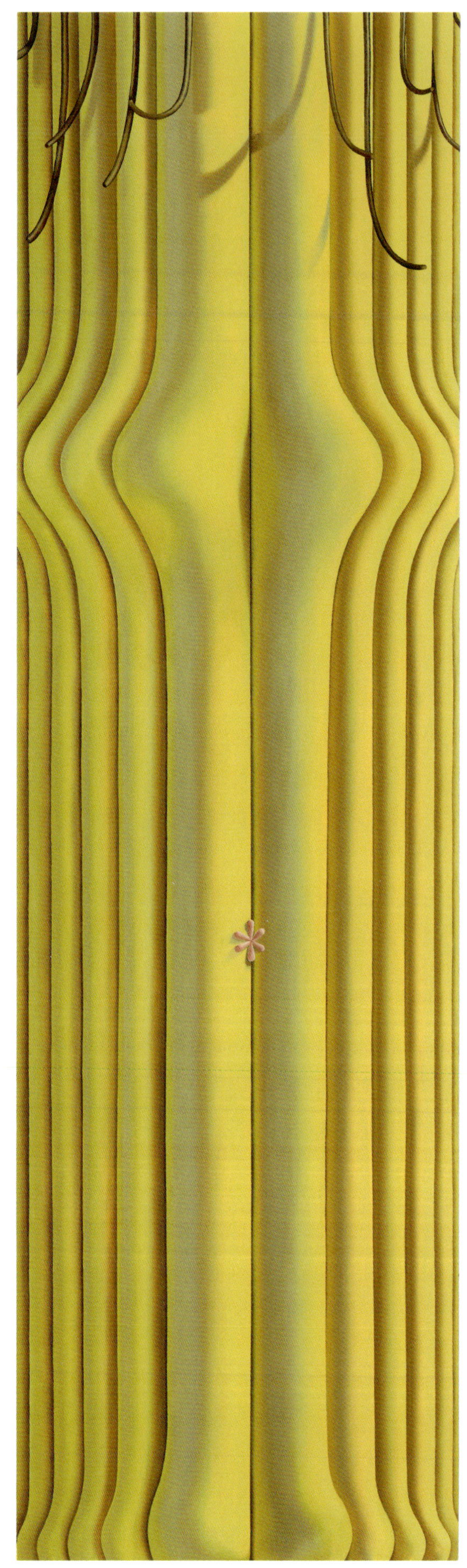

    Herm, 2016

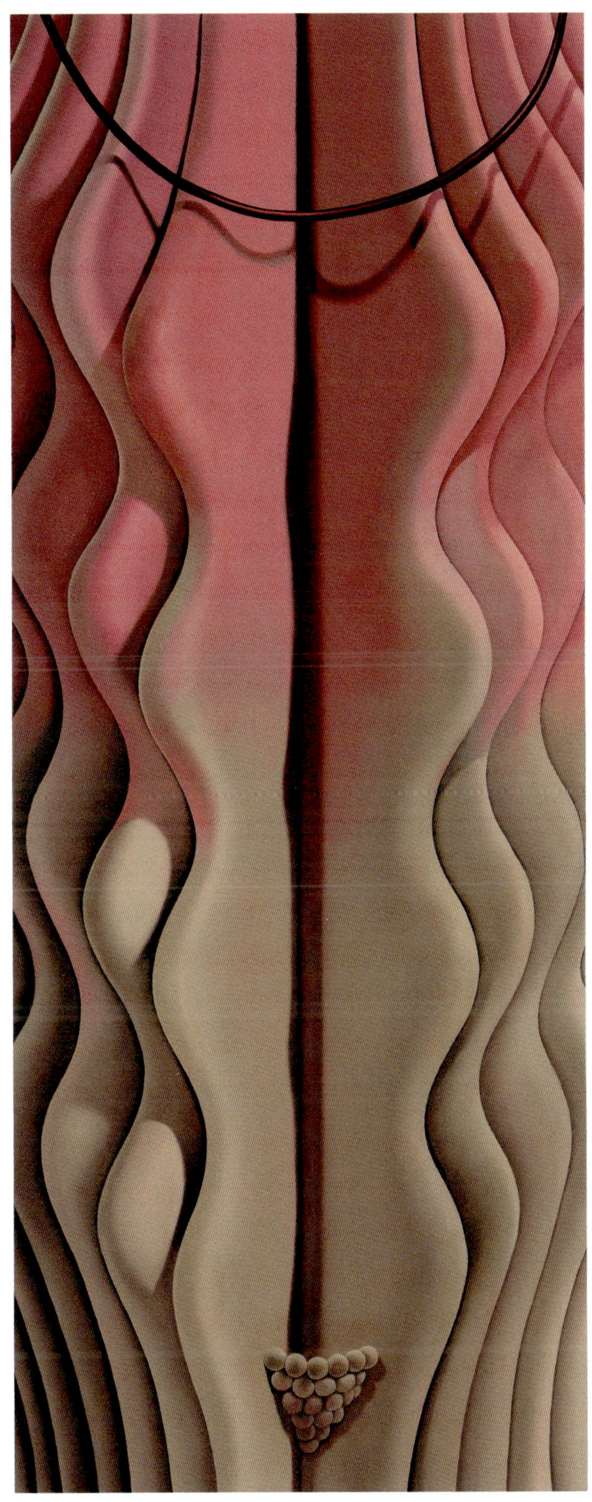

Herm 2, 2016

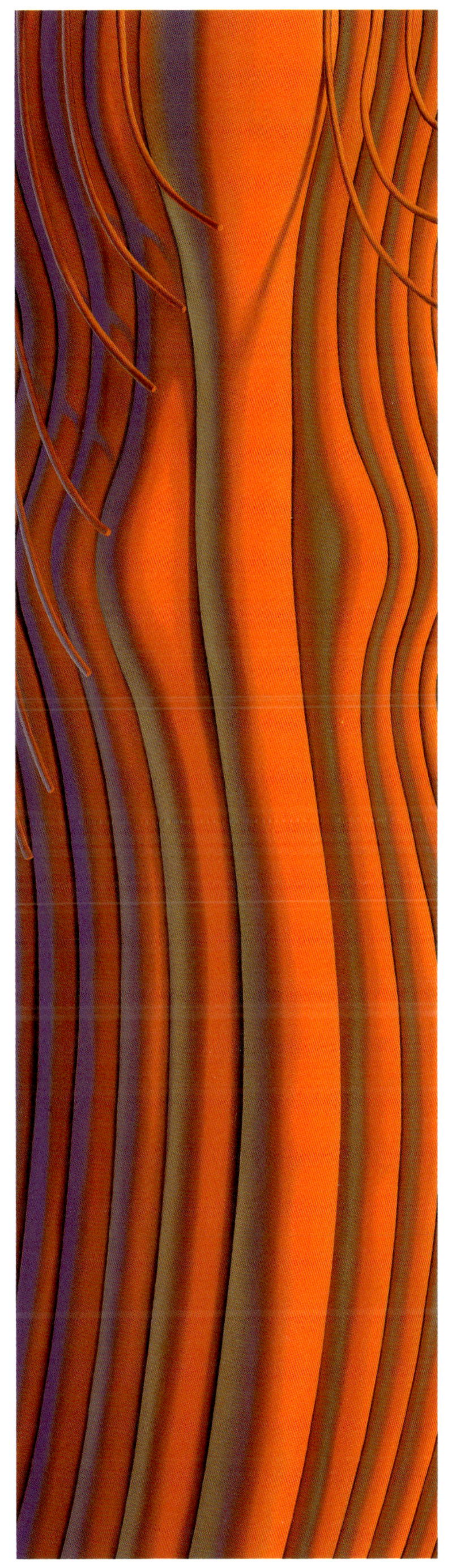

Herm 3, 2016

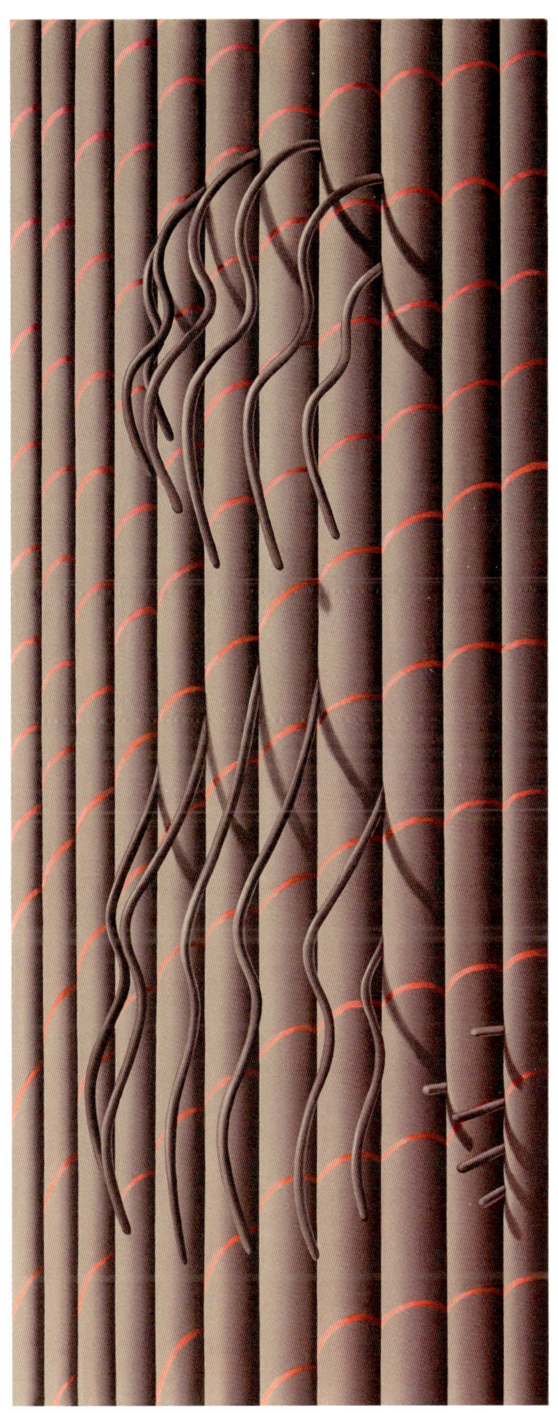

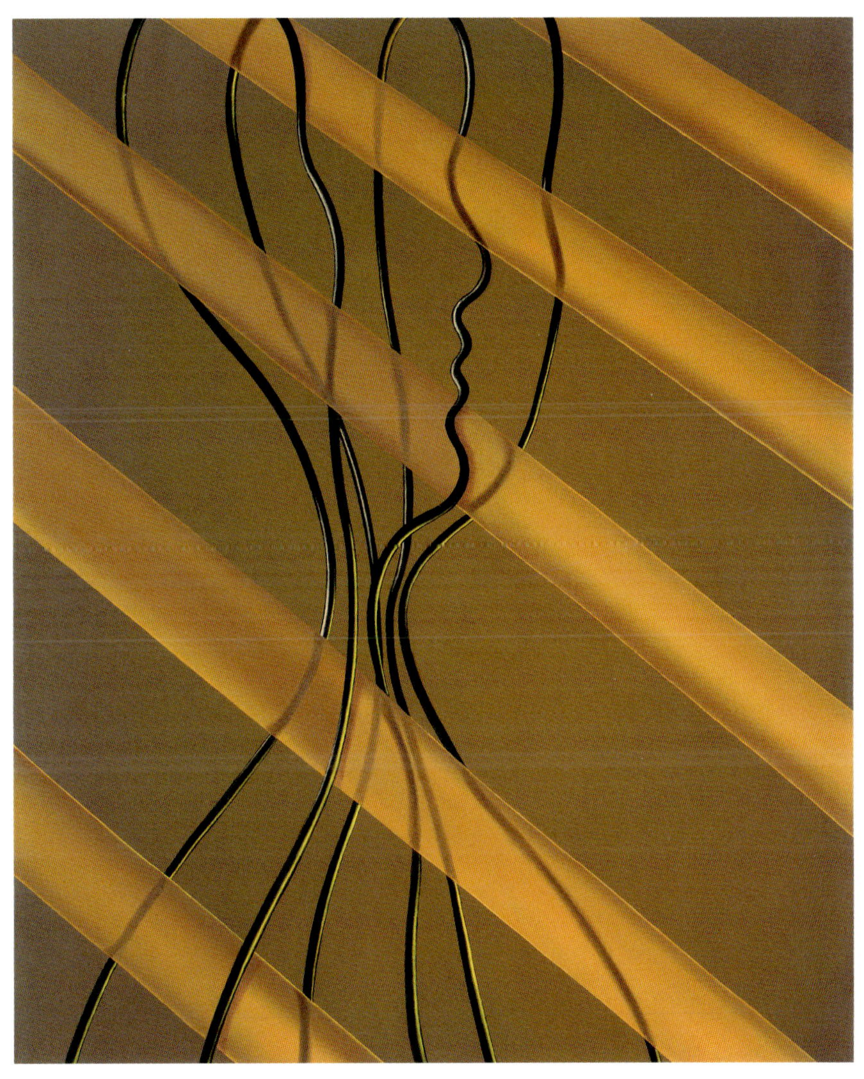

Scrim 2, 2016

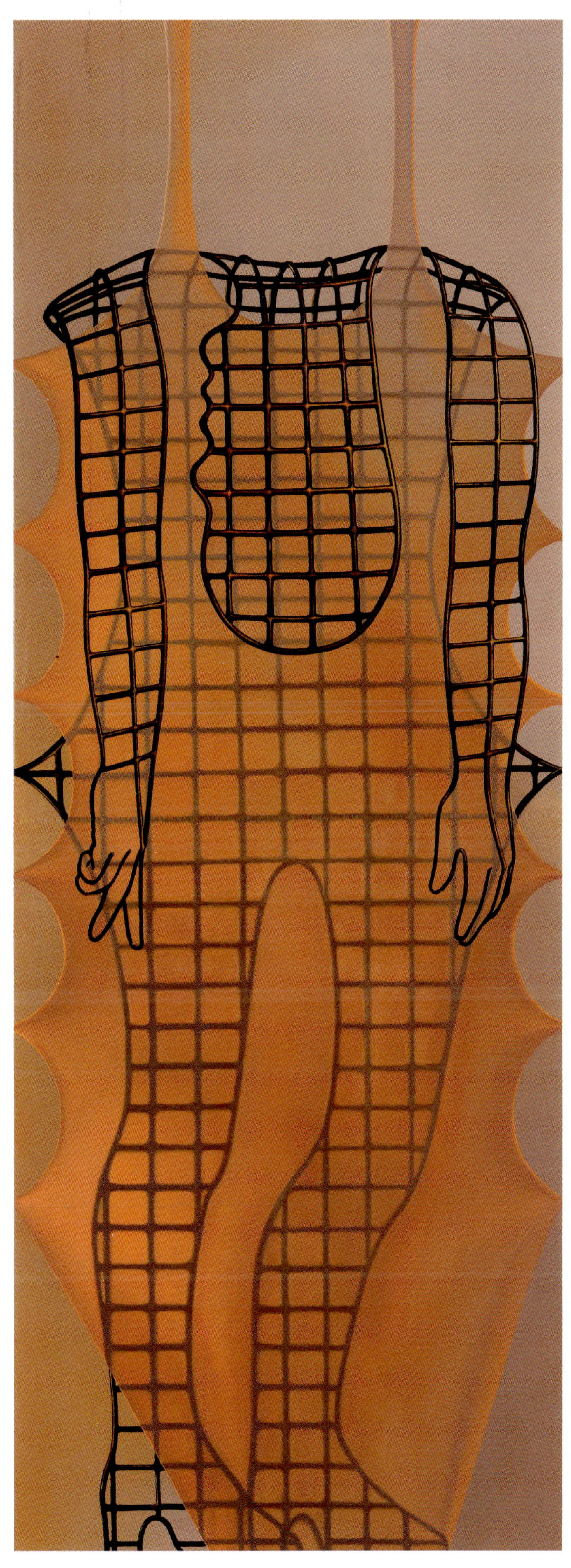

Scrim, 2016

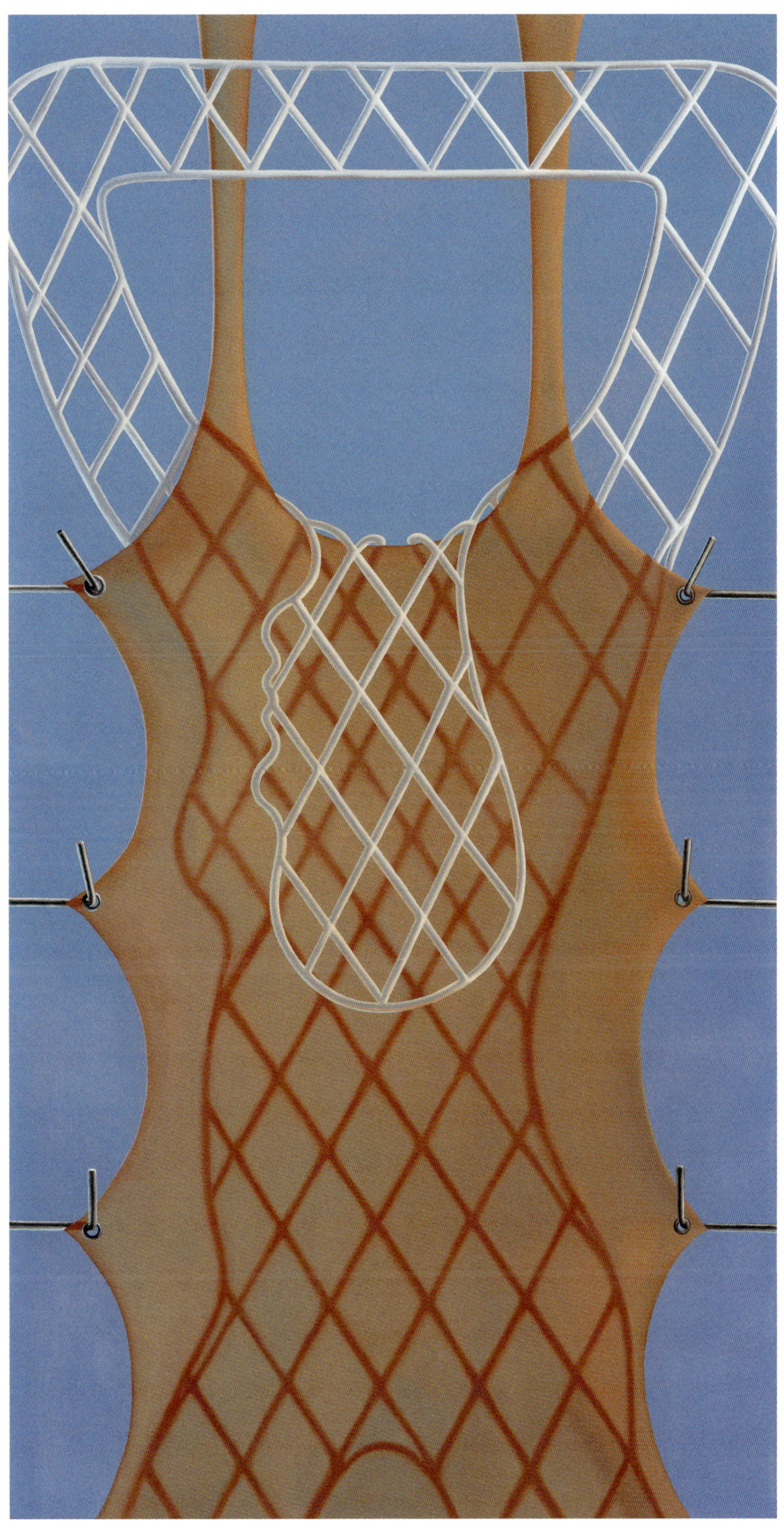

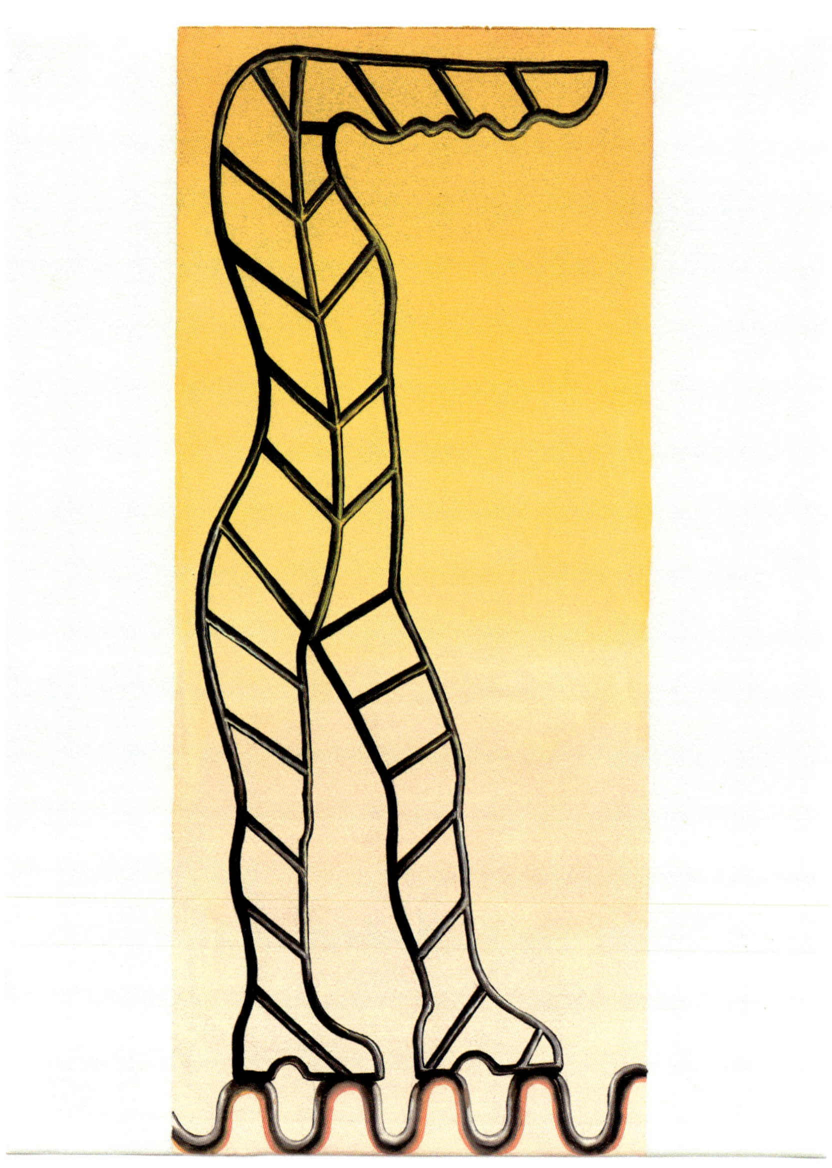

106   *Study for 'Backbone' 1, 2016*

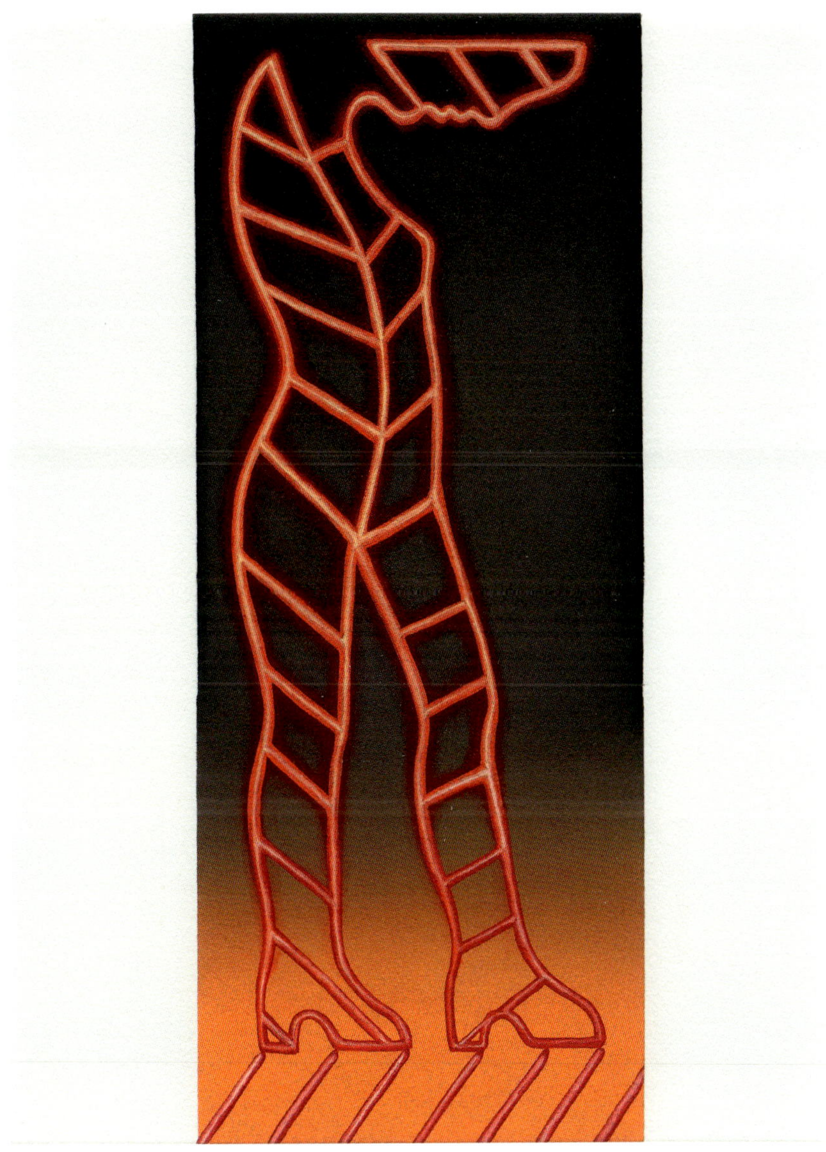

Study for 'Backbone' 2, 2016

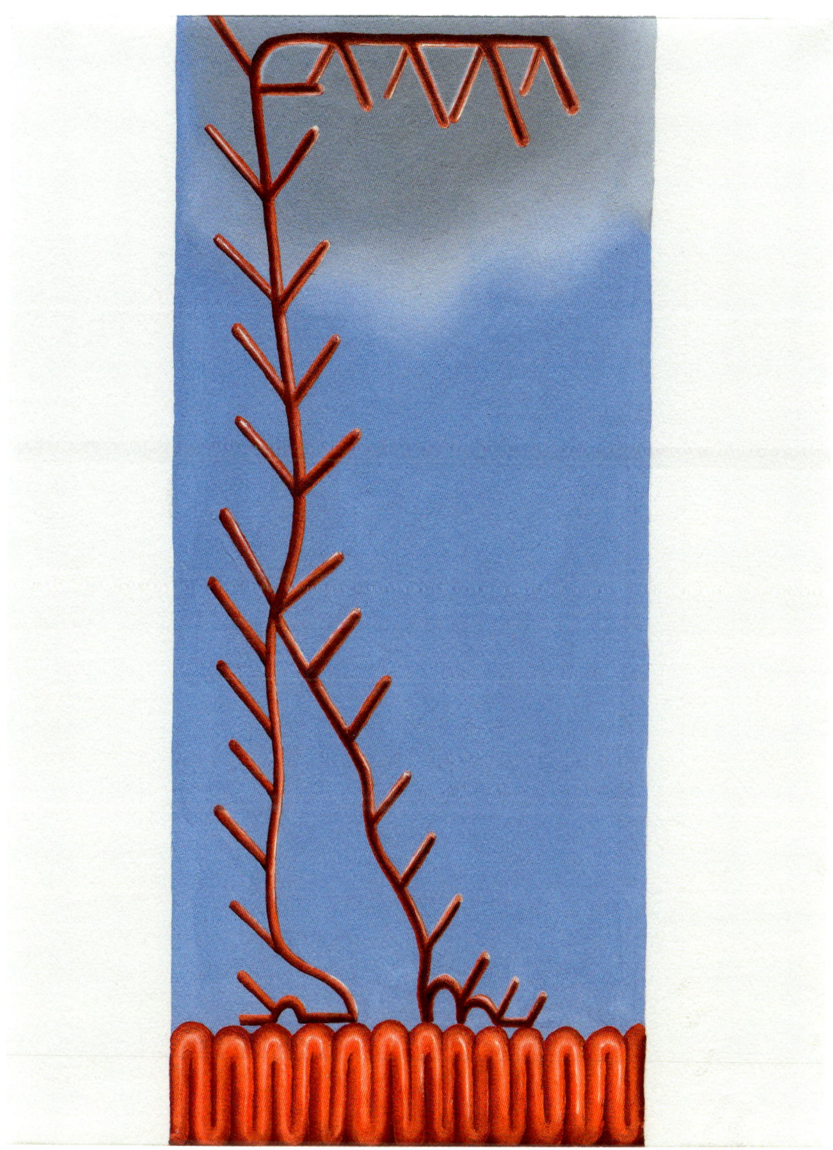

Untitled, 2016

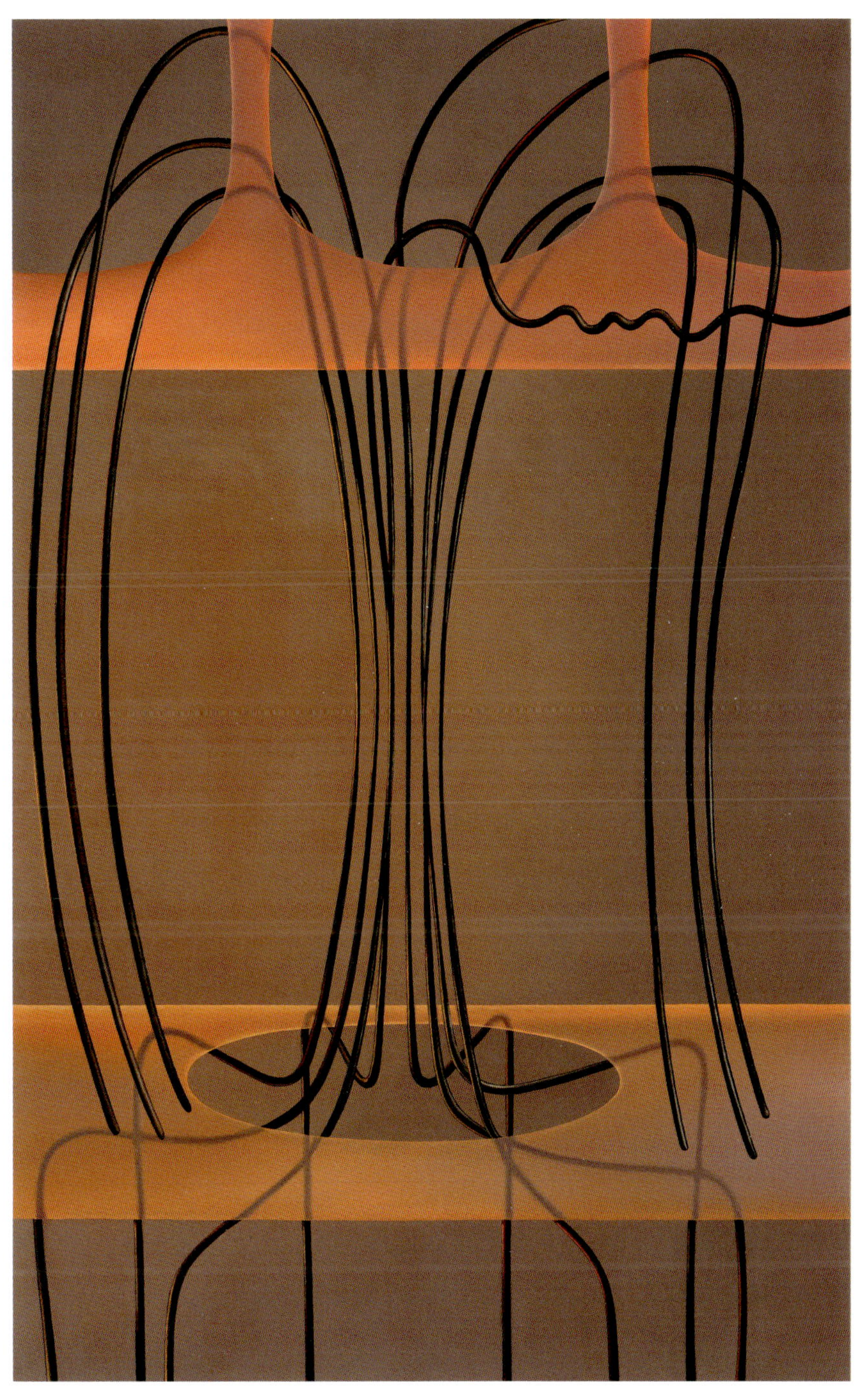

Stays, 2016

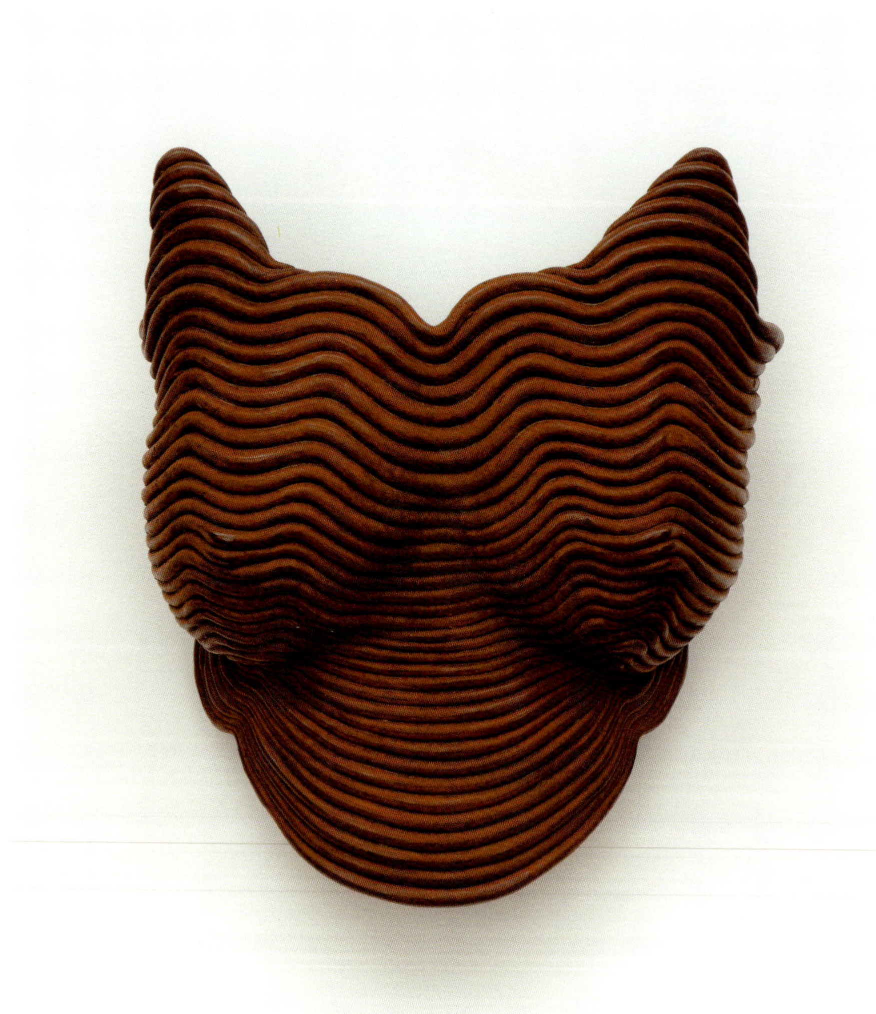

110   *Cuirasse*, 2016

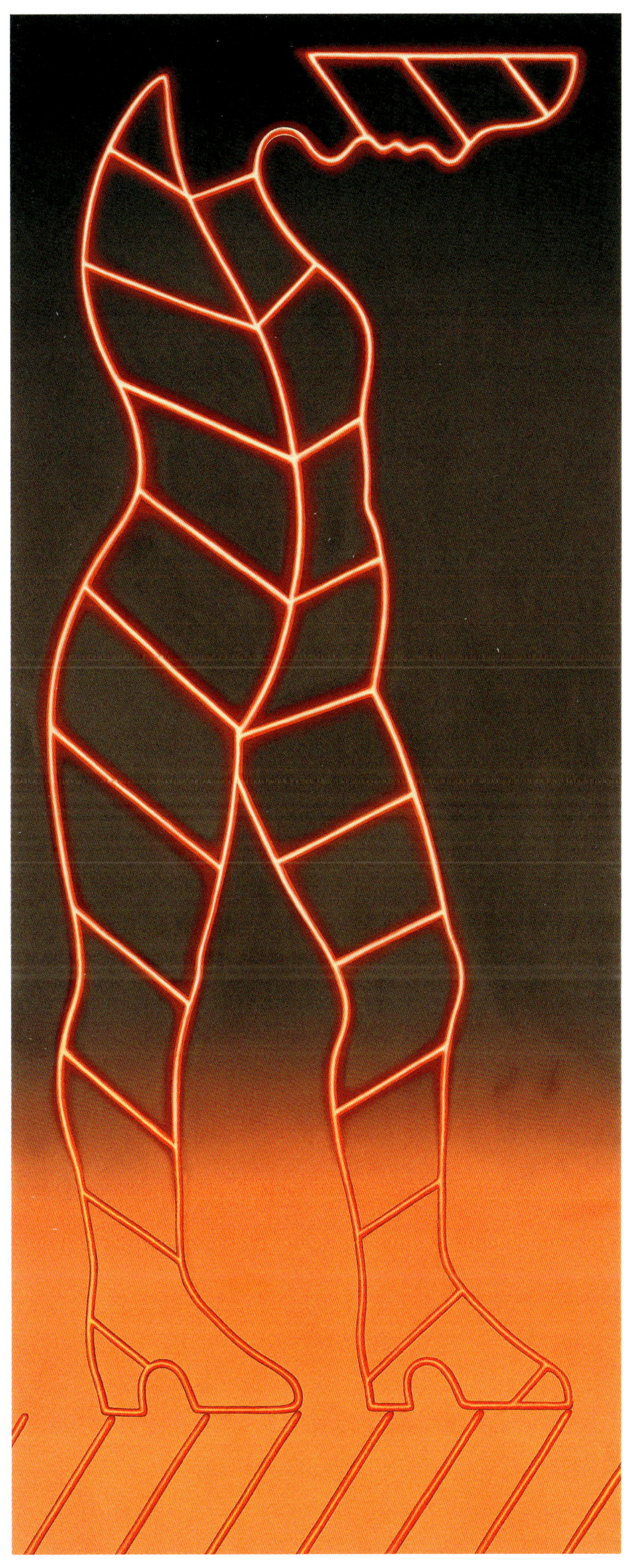

Backbone, 2016

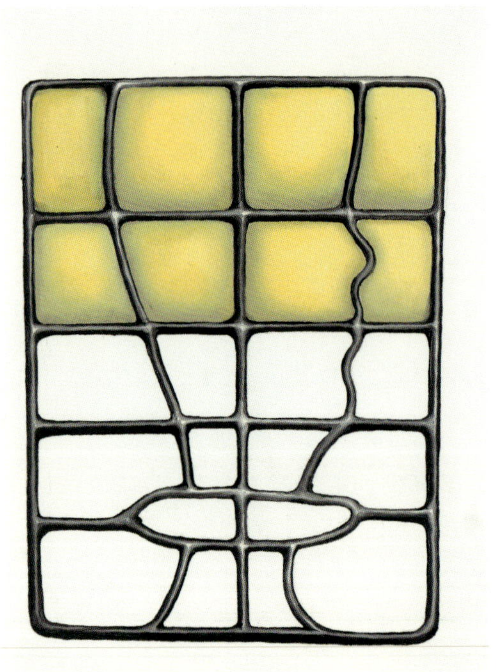

     Untitled, 2016

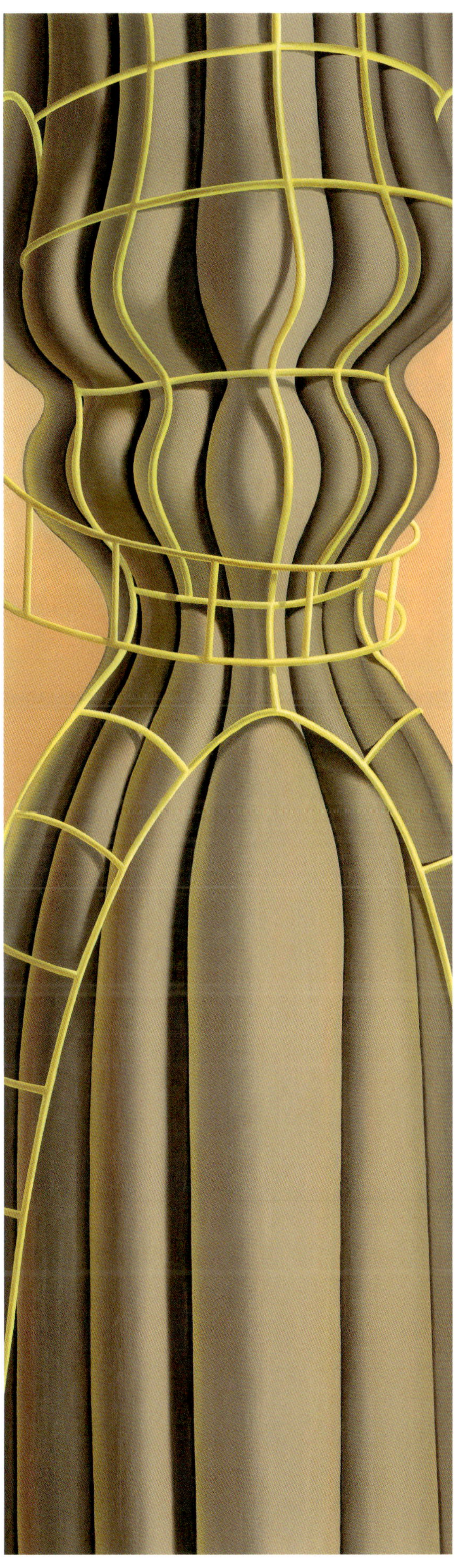

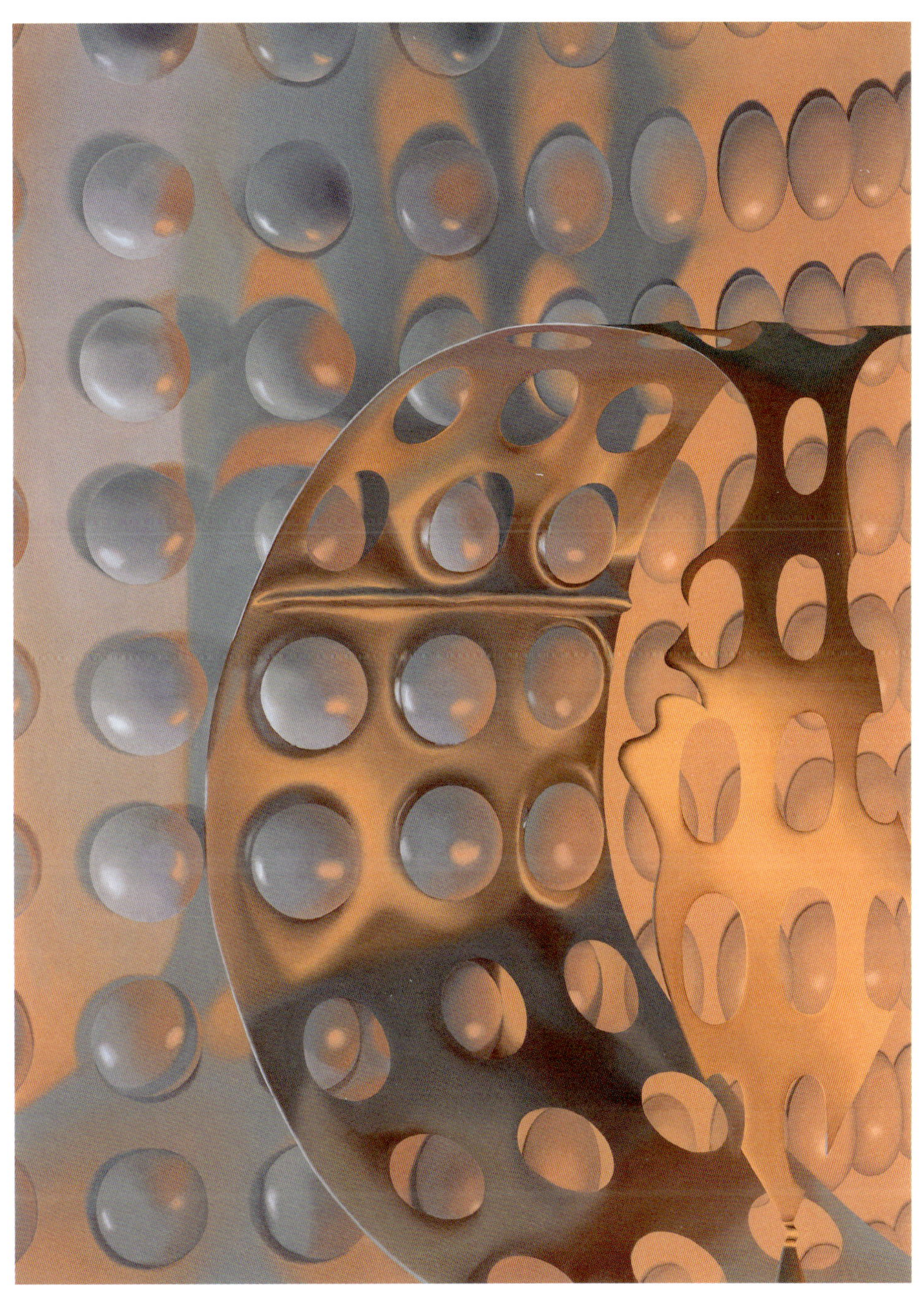

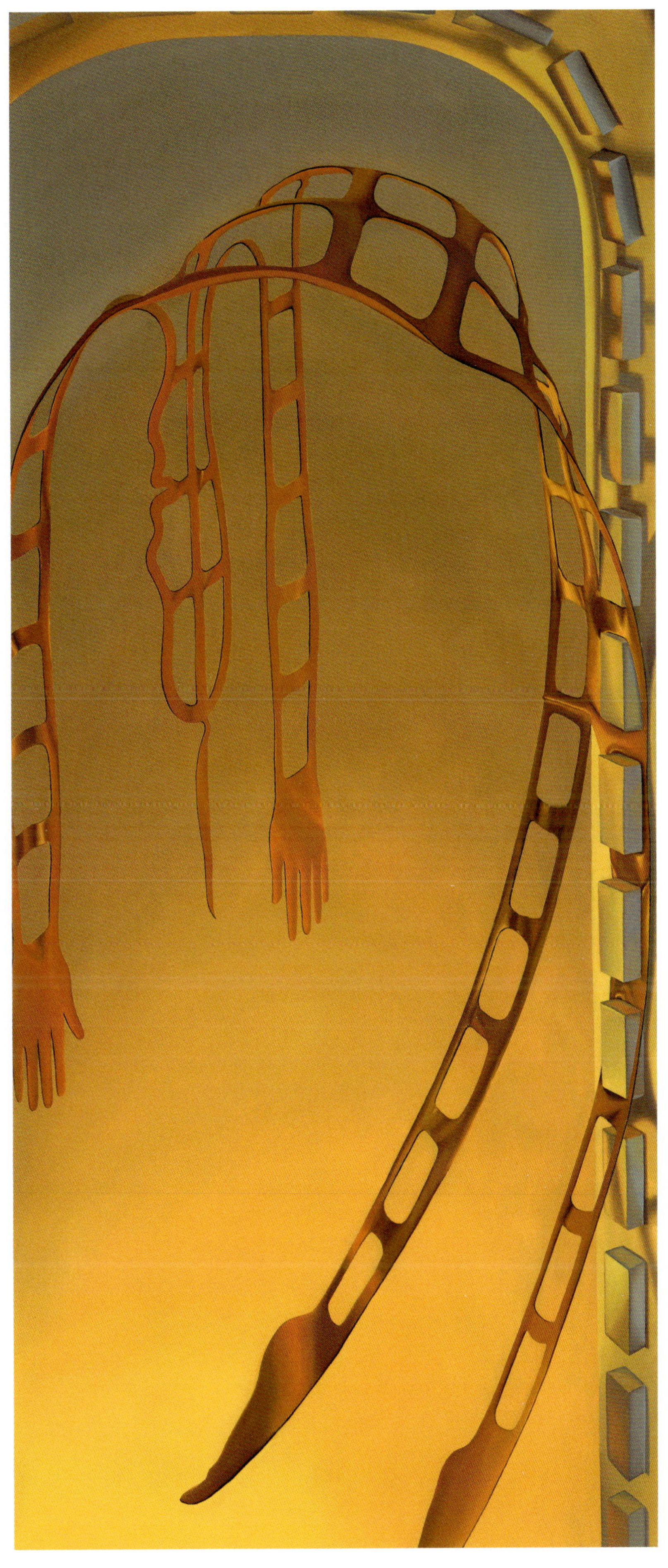

Free Peel 2, 2017

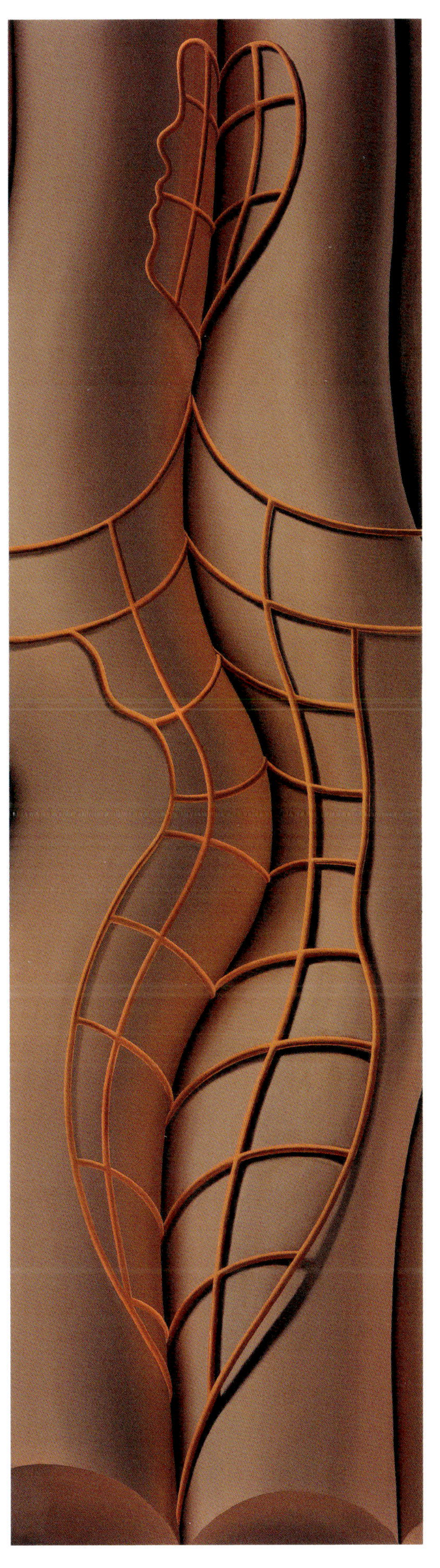

Writhes, 2017

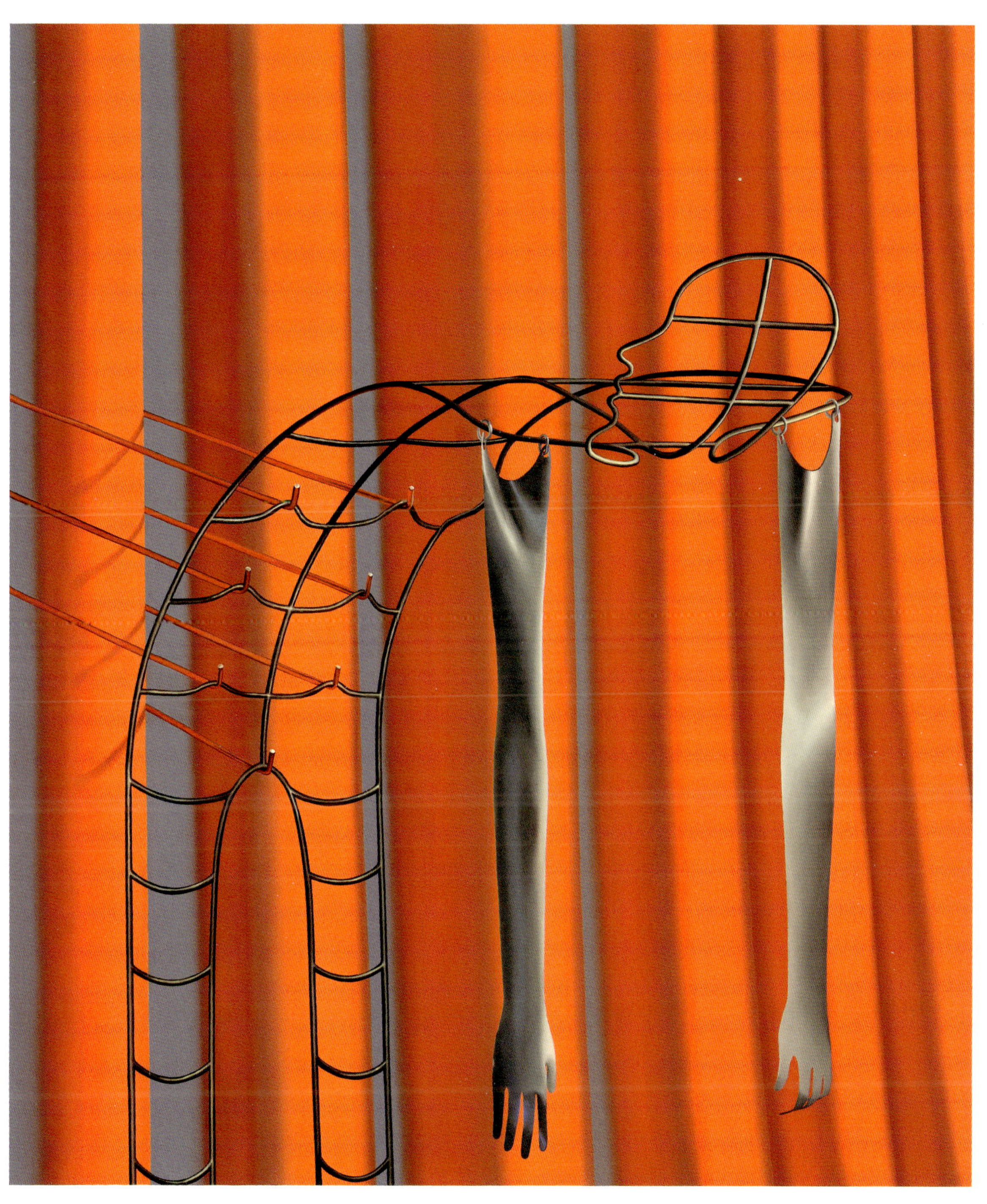

Unseen Forces, 2017

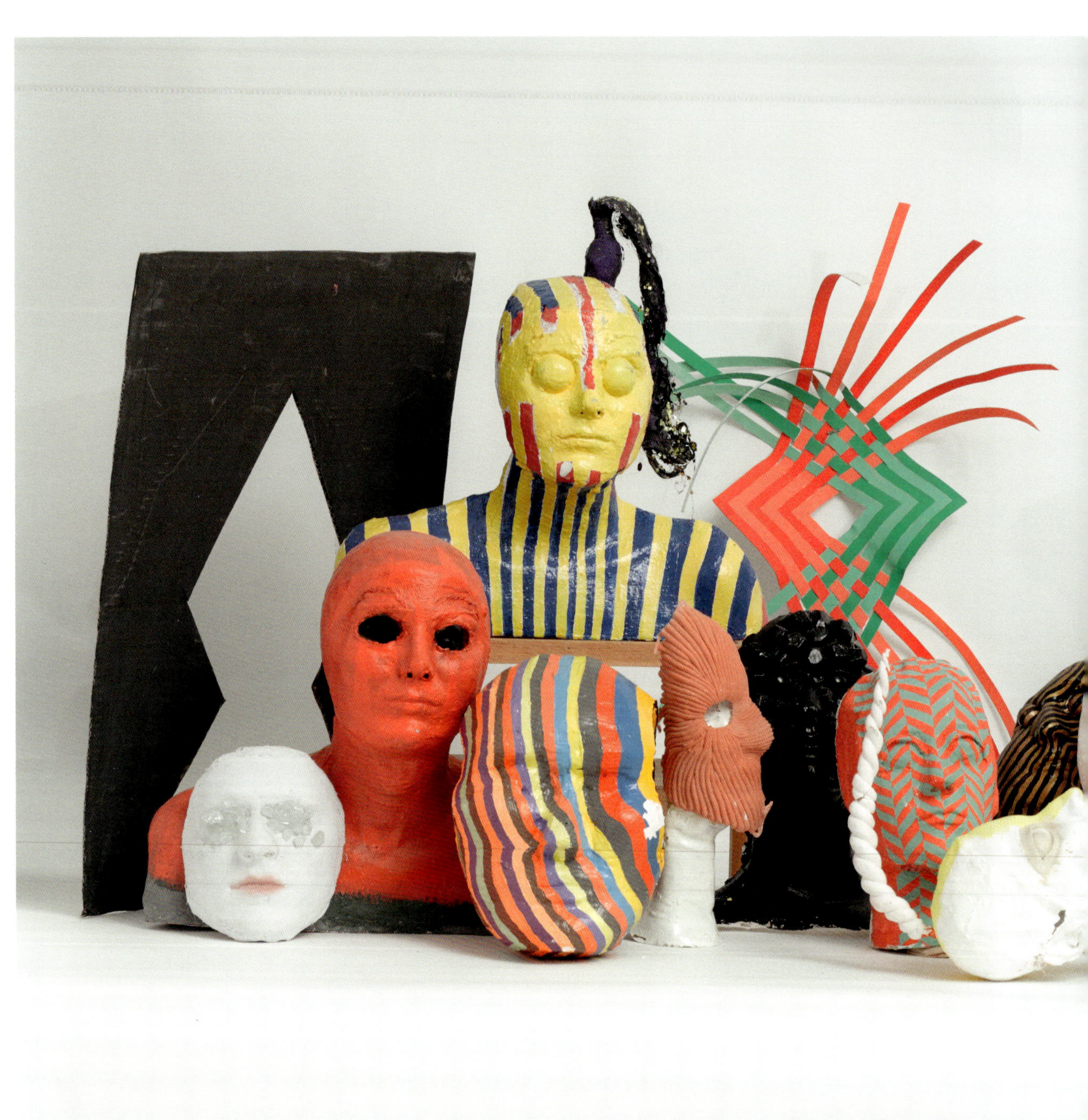

  Painting Props, 2009–2016

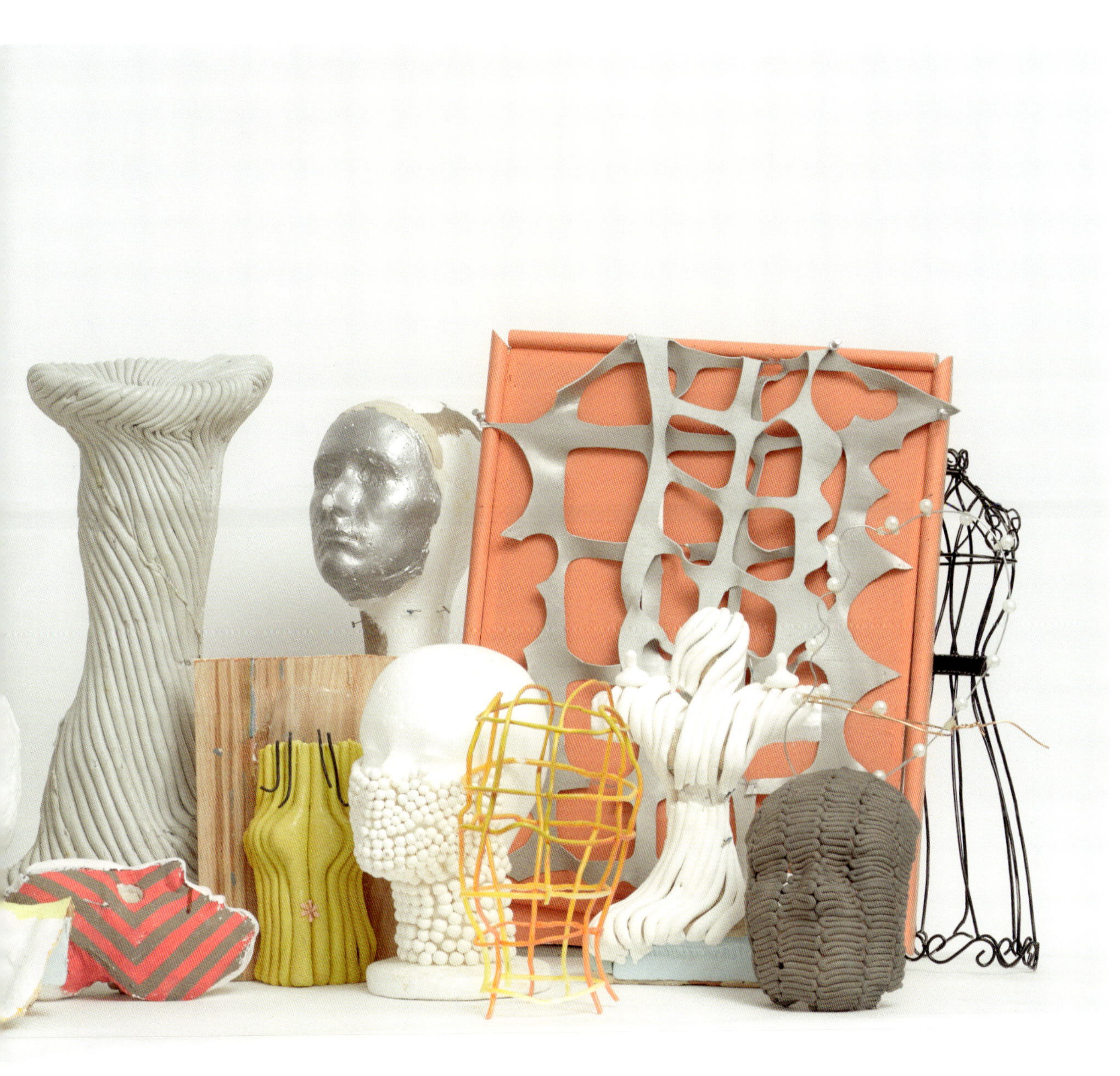

Captions

Studs, 2006
Oil on canvas
20 × 23 ½ in.
(50.8 × 59.7 cm)

No Solutions, 2009
Oil on canvas over panel
24 × 30 in.
(60.96 × 76.20 cm)
Photo: Mark Woods

Sequins, 2010
Oil on canvas over panel
20 × 16 in.
(50.80 × 40.64 cm)
Photo: Mark Woods

Goldwarp, 2010
Oil on canvas over panel
18 × 14 in.
(45.72 × 35.56 cm)
Photo: Luc Demers

Untitled, 2011
Oil on canvas over panel
20 × 16 in.
(50.8 × 40.6 cm.)
Photo: Mark Woods

Coverage, 2011
Oil on canvas over panel
22 × 15 in.
(55.88 × 38.10 cm)
Photo: Mark Woods
Zabludowicz Collection, London

Chameleon, 2011
Oil on linen
24 × 20 in.
(60.96 × 50.80 cm)
Photo: Mark Woods

Coils, 2011
Oil on canvas
24 × 22 in.
(60.96 × 55.88 cm)
Photo: Mark Woods

Carapace, 2011
Oil on canvas over panel
24 × 20 in.
(60.96 × 50.80 cm)
Photo: Joshua White/China
Art Objects

Lashes, 2011
Oil on canvas over panel
22 × 18 in.
(55.88 × 45.72 cm)
Photo: Mark Woods
Zabludowicz Collection, London

Untitled, 2011
Oil on canvas over panel
19 × 17 in.
(48.3 × 43.2 cm.)
Photo: Luc Demers

Collared, 2011
Oil on canvas over panel
24 × 20 in.
(60.96 × 50.80 cm)
Photo: Luc Demers

Bossy Pins, 2012
Oil on canvas over panel
24 × 22 in.
(60.96 × 55.88 cm)
Photo: Mark Woods

Claude, 2012
Acryla-gouache on panel
16 × 12 in.
(40.64 × 30.48 cm)
Photo: Mark Woods

Herringbone, 2011
Acryla-gouache on paper
12 × 9 in. (30.48 × 22.86 cm)
Photo: Mark Woods

Prop, 2012
Oil on canvas over panel
24 × 18 in.
(60.96 × 45.72 cm)
Photo: Mark Woods

Strange Maine, 2012
Oil on canvas over panel
30 × 22 in.
(76.20 × 55.88 cm)
Photo: Mark Woods

Frotteur, 2012
Oil on canvas over panel
30 × 22 in.
(76.20 × 55.88 cm)
Photo: Mark Woods

Nets, 2012
Acryla-gouache on paper
14 × 10 in.
(35.56 × 25.40 cm)
Photo: Mark Woods

Blue Loomer, 2013
Oil on canvas over panel
32 × 24 in.
(81.28 × 60.96 cm)
Photo: Mark Woods

Rolling Shutter 2, 2013
Oil on canvas over panel
30 x 19 in.
(76.2 x 48.26 cm.)
Photo: Luc Demers

Bottom Feeder, 2015
Oil and acrylic on linen
and wood
20 ½ × 16 in.
(52.07 × 40.64 cm)
Photo: Luc Demers

Orange Sucker, 2014
Oil on canvas over panel
20 × 16 in.
(50.80 × 40.64 cm)
Photo: Luc Demers

Veined, Cuffed, Brained 1, 2013
Oil on canvas
14 × 11 in.
(35.56 × 27.94 cm)
Photo: Luc Demers

Veined, Cuffed, Brained 2, 2013
Oil on linen over panel
14 × 11 in.
(35.56 × 27.94 cm)
Photo: Luc Demers

Bridle, 2013
Oil on canvas over panel
25 × 22 in.
(63.50 × 55.88 cm)
Photo: Luc Demers

Shade, 2014
Oil on linen over panel
30 × 20 in.
(76.20 × 50.80 cm)
Photo: Luc Demers

Feeder, 2014
Oil on linen over panel
31 × 16 in.
(78.74 × 40.64 cm)
Photo: Mark Woods

Strider 2, 2014
Oil on linen over panel
33 × 24 in.
(83.82 × 60.96 cm)
Photo: Mark Woods

Squirm, 2014
Oil on linen over panel
25 × 19 in.
(63.50 × 48.26 cm)
Photo: Luc Demers

Motes, 2015
Oil on linen over panel
19 ½ × 13 ½ in.
(49.53 × 34.29 cm)
Photo: Luc Demers

Chur, 2014
Oil on linen over panel
24 × 18 in.
(60.96 × 45.72 cm)
Photo: Luc Demers
Collection of Baltimore
Museum of Art

Valance, 2014/2015
Oil on linen over panel
30 × 20 in.
(76.20 × 50.80 cm)
Photo: Mark Woods

Monad, 2014
Oil on linen over panel
25 × 19 in.
(63.50 × 48.26 cm)
Photo: Mark Woods
Collection of NGV, Melbourne

Troll, 2014
Oil on linen over panel
15 × 12 in.
(38.10 × 30.48 cm)
Photo: Mark Woods
Collection of NGV, Melbourne

Saccades, 2014
Oil on linen over panel
17 ½ × 15 in.
(44.45 × 38.10 cm)
Photo: Mark Woods
Collection of NGV, Melbourne

Chur, 2014/15
Bronze
9 × 6 × 4 ½ in.
(22.86 × 15.24 × 11.43 cm)
Photo: Mark Woods

Marker, 2015
Oil on linen over panel
25 × 19 in.
(63.50 × 48.26 cm)
Photo: Mark Woods

Reef, 2015
Oil on linen over panel
12 in. diameter
(30.48 cm. diameter)
Photo: Mark Woods

Field, 2014
Oil on gessoed panel
11 ¼ in. diameter
(28.58 cm)
Photo: Luc Demers

Hilt, 2015
Oil on linen over panel
32 × 21 in.
(81.28 × 53.34 cm)
Photo: Mark Woods

Rebecca, 2015
Oil on linen over panel
36 × 24 in.
(91.44 × 60.96 cm)
Photo: Luc Demers

Hide, 2015
Oil on linen over panel
42 ¾ × 19 in.
(108.58 × 48.26 cm)
Photo: Mark Woods

Warm Leatherette, 2015
Oil on linen over panel
29 × 26 ½ in.
(73.66 × 67.31 cm)
Photo: Johan Blommaert

La Maitresse, 2015
Oil on linen over panel
44 × 20 in.
(111.76 × 50.80 cm)
Photo: Luc Demers

Herm, 2016
Oil on linen over panel
48 × 14 in.
(121.92 × 35.56 cm)
Photo: Mark Woods

Herm 2, 2016
Oil on linen over panel
38 × 13 ¼ in.
(96.52 × 33.66 cm)
Photo: Mark Woods
Collection of NGV, Melbourne

Herm 3, 2016
Oil on linen over panel
45 × 12 ¾ in.
(114.30 × 32.38 cm)
Photo: Mark Woods

Pillar, 2015
Oil on linen over panel
38 × 15 in.
(96.52 × 38.10 cm)
Photo: Luc Demers

Scrim 2, 2016
Oil on linen over panel
24 × 20 in.
(60.96 × 50.80 cm)
Photo: Mark Woods

Scrim, 2016
Oil on linen over panel
51 × 19 in.
(129.54 × 48.26 cm)
Photo: Mark Woods

Tenterhooks, 2016
Oil on linen over panel
38 × 20 in.
(96.52 × 50.80 cm)
Photo: Mark Woods

Study for 'Backbone' 1, 2016
Oil on Arches Oil Paper
16 × 11 ⅛ in.
(40.64 × 28.26 cm)
Photo: Mark Woods

Study for 'Backbone' 2, 2016
Oil on Arches Oil Paper
16 × 11 ⅛ in.
(40.64 × 28.26 cm)
Photo: Mark Woods

Untitled, 2016
Oil on Arches Oil Paper
16 × 11 ⅛ in.
(40.64 × 28.26 cm)
Photo: Mark Woods

Stays, 2016
Oil on linen over panel
24 x 38 in.
(60.96 x 96.52 cm)
Photo: Mark Woods

Cuirasse, 2016
Cast bronze with red brick patina
12 ½ × 11 × 3 ⁹⁄₁₀ in
(31.75 × 28 × 10 cm)
Photo by Mark Woods

Backbone, 2016
Oil on linen over panel
54 × 22 in.
(137.16 × 55.88 cm)
Photo: Mark Woods

Untitled, 2016
Oil on Arches Oil Paper
12 ⅛ × 9 in.
(30.8 × 22.86 cm)
Photo: Mark Woods

Cinch, 2016
Oil on linen over panel
50 × 15 in.
(127 × 38.1 cm)
Photo: Mark Woods

Free Peel, 2016
Oil on linen over panel
30 × 22 in.
(76.2 × 55.88 cm)
Photo: Mark Woods

Free Peel 2, 2017
Oil on linen over panel
58 × 25 in.
(147.32 × 63.5 cm)
Photo: Mark Woods

Writhes, 2017
Oil on linen over panel
50 × 14 in.
(127 × 35.56 cm)
Photo: Mark Woods

Unseen Forces, 2017
Oil on linen over panel
42 × 36 in.
(106.68 × 91.44 cm)
Photo: Mark Woods

FIRST EDITION 1000

ISBN 978-0-692-84247-8

DESIGN BY Familiar
PUBLISHED BY Foxy Production

Many thanks to Mark and Judy Bednar, Jeffrey Deitch,
Lonti Ebers, Scott J. Lorinsky, Adam and Iris Singer, and
Gary Tenen for their generous support of this publication.

All works are in private collections unless otherwise noted.

Printed in Germany.